# Quotes to Level Up Your Life:

## 1000+ Inspirational Quotes to Boost Wisdom, Creativity & Growth

by KW Mackey

This edition fist published in 2023 by Rational Publishing at www.rationalpublishing.com

Copyright © 2023 by KW Mackey

All rights reserved. No part of this publication may be reproduced or transmitted in any form or by any means, electronic or mechanical, including photocopying, recording, or by any information storage and retrieval system, without permission in writing from Rational Publishing, reviewers may quote brief passages.

ISBN: 979-8-9885199-0-4  (Hardback)
ISBN: 979-8-9885199-1-1  (Paperback)
ISBN: 979-8-9885199-2-8  (E-book)
ISBN: 979-8-9885199-3-5  (Pocket Reference)

Library of Congress Cataloging-in-Publication Data available upon request

Typeset and Cover Design by Rational Publishing

# Table of Contents

## Self-Discovery ................................................................ 1
- Identity and Purpose ........................................... 1
- Emotional Intelligence ......................................... 6
- Personal Values ................................................. 10
- Mindfulness ....................................................... 15
- Self-Acceptance ................................................. 19

## Overcoming .................................................................. 25
- Facing Adversity ................................................ 25
- Courage & Perseverance ..................................... 30
- Acceptance & Personal Growth ............................ 34
- Overcoming Fear ................................................ 38
- Hopefulness ....................................................... 42

## Relationships ................................................................ 47
- Building Trust .................................................... 47
- Communication .................................................. 50
- Support and Encouragement ............................... 54
- Resolving Conflict .............................................. 58
- Appreciation and Gratitude ................................. 61
- Character, Empathy, and Love ............................. 66

## Habits ......................................................................... 74
- Developing Good Habits ..................................... 74
- Breaking Bad Habits ........................................... 79
- Discipline & Consistency .................................... 84
- Habit & Character .............................................. 87
- Long-term Impact .............................................. 90

## Leadership .................................................................. 96
- Inspiring Others ................................................. 96
- Vision & Strategy ............................................... 100
- Empowerment & Teamwork ................................. 103

- Decision-making.................................................................108
- Leading by Example...........................................................113
- Dealing with Opposition.....................................................116

# Learning.................................................................................121
- The Value of Education.....................................................121
- Lifelong Learning................................................................125
- Learning from Failure.......................................................130
- Teaching and Mentorship.................................................133
- Attaining Knowledge........................................................137
- Curiosity and Critical Thinking .......................................141

# Growth..................................................................................146
- Personal Development.....................................................146
- Facing Obstacles & Embracing Change........................150
- Goal Setting and Achievement........................................155
- Building Resilience............................................................160
- Positive Thinking...............................................................164

# Focus & Clarity...................................................................169
- Clear Thinking...................................................................169
- Decision Making...............................................................173
- Focus & Concentration....................................................177
- Purpose and Intention......................................................181
- Mindfulness & Awareness................................................187

# Creativity.............................................................................193
- Imagination & Innovation...............................................193
- Artistic Expression............................................................198
- Embracing Originality......................................................203
- The Creative Process & Mindset....................................208
- Creative Inspiration..........................................................211

# Productivity........................................................................218
- Taking Action & Prioritizing...........................................218
- Time Management & Efficiency....................................223
- Perseverance & Resilience...............................................228

    Mindset and Focus..................................................................232
    Balance and Simplicity...........................................................237

# Virtue & Character..................................................242
    Integrity & Honesty................................................................242
    Kindness & Compassion........................................................246
    Courage & Bravery.................................................................249
    Humility & Modesty...............................................................252
    Responsibility & Accountability............................................255
    Patience & Persistence...........................................................260
    Wisdom and Discipline..........................................................263
    Freedom & Hope.....................................................................268
    Virtue & Character..................................................................270

# Acknowledgments.................................................278

# Preface

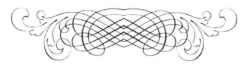

Throughout life, we face challenges and uncertainties. Many rely on trial and error, occasionally receiving advice from a friend. Unfortunately, not everyone has access to consistent guidance. If you've ever needed wisdom to navigate life's complexities, here's the book for you. It provides timeless guidance on how to handle adversity, build strong relationships, and make wise decisions. It's a must-read for anyone looking to gain clarity and confidence in their life.

"Quotes to Level Up Your Life" aims to be that invaluable source of knowledge, offering the insight you need to conquer challenges and illuminate the unknown. This collection of 1000+ (actually over 1200) wise sayings from across time and cultures serves as a beacon to help you navigate life with confidence and resilience. Let these quotes inspire, motivate, and elevate your understanding, empowering you to live a life enriched by the wisdom of the ages.

Whether you're seeking a gentle nudge in the right direction or a powerful catalyst for transformation, "Quotes to Level Up Your Life" is the perfect companion. Keep this book by your side, and let it serve as your guide and inspiration as you strive for personal growth and unlock your full potential.

# Dedication

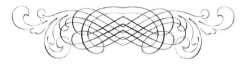

To my son, may these quotes serve as a guiding lighthouse, illuminating the way through life's foggy seas.

## Identity and Purpose

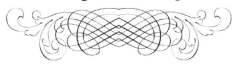

A person's identity refers to the unique combination of characteristics, beliefs, values, experiences, and affiliations that define who they are as an individual. This section contains inspiring quotes that focus on the journey of self-discovery, embracing one's identity, and finding a sense of purpose in life. These powerful words of wisdom remind us of the importance of knowing who we are and staying true to ourselves as we navigate the complexities of life.

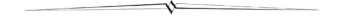

"We live our lives forward, but we understand our lives backward."
- Søren Kierkegaard

"Conquer yourself rather than the world."
- Rene Descartes

## Self-Discovery

"The best way to find yourself is to lose yourself in the service of others."
- Mahatma Gandhi

"You become what you believe."
- Oprah Winfrey

"If my life is going to mean anything. I have to live it myself."
- Rick Riordan

"The will is never free - it is always attached to an object, a purpose. It is simply the engine in the car - it can't steer."
- Joyce Cary 1888-1957 Sartor Resartus

"Talent is what a man possesses and genius what possesses man."
- Isaac Stern quoting a famous english writer 1983

"We shape clay into a pot, but it is the emptiness inside that holds whatever we want."
- Tao Te Ching

"Your sole contribution to the sum of things is yourself."
- Frank Crane

"The privilege of a lifetime is to become who you truly are."
- Carl Gustav Jung

"What lies behind us and what lies before us are tiny matters compared to what lies within us."
- Ralph Waldo Emerson

# Self-Discovery

"Your real self may be hiding somewhere, look for it within, when you find yourself, you can freely be what you want to be."
- Michael Bassey Johnson

"Only when we face the impossible and experience the unbearable do we find out who we truly are."
- Vironika Tugaleva

"To find yourself, think for yourself."
- Socrates

"Find out who you are and do it on purpose."
- Dolly Parton

"The most difficult thing in life is to know yourself."
- Thales of Miletus

"The most important kind of freedom is to be what you really are."
- Jim Morrison

"Discovering who you are today is the first step to being who you will be tomorrow."
- Destiny's Odyssey

"When I discover who I am, I'll be free."
- Ralph Ellison, Invisible Man

"Be yourself; everyone else is already taken."
- Oscar Wilde

Self-Discovery

"Never be bullied into silence. Never allow yourself to be made a victim. Accept no one's definition of your life; define yourself."
    - Harvey Fierstein

"Find out who you are and be that person. That's what your soul was put on this Earth to be. Find that truth, live that truth, and everything else will come."
    - Ellen DeGeneres

"The hardest challenge is to be yourself in a world where everyone is trying to make you be somebody else."
    - E. E. Cummings

"Life is not about finding yourself. Life is about creating yourself."
    - Lolly Daskal

"Be yourself; there's no one better qualified."
    - Anthony J. D'Angelo

"The only person you are destined to become is the person you decide to be."
    - Ralph Waldo Emerson

"Be yourself, for if you're not yourself, who will be?"
    - Benjamin Franklin

"By being yourself, you put something wonderful in the world that was not there before."
    - Edwin Elliot

## Self-Discovery

"Have the courage to follow your heart and intuition. They somehow already know what you truly want to become. Everything else is secondary."
- Steve Jobs

"To know yourself is the first and most important step in pursuing your dreams and goals."
- Stedman Graham

"Only when you are aware of your true nature can you fully express your unique gifts and talents."
- unknown

"Find your authentic self, and you will find your true purpose in life."
- Deepak Chopra

"Self-discovery is the process of learning more about yourself and who you are. This can lead to personal growth and a more fulfilling life."
- unknown

"Your journey to self-discovery will be filled with challenges and triumphs. Embrace them all, for they will shape you into the person you are meant to be."
- unknown

"Self-discovery is a journey that leads us to a deeper understanding of ourselves, our values, and our purpose."
- unknown

Self-Discovery

"Sometimes, you have to lose yourself to find yourself."
   - unknown

"Self-discovery is the key to unlocking your full potential and living a life of purpose, passion, and fulfillment."
   - unknown

## Emotional Intelligence

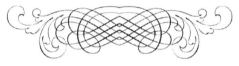

Emotional intelligence refers to the ability to recognize, understand, and manage emotions, both in oneself and others. It involves being aware of one's own emotions, being able to express them appropriately, and effectively handling interpersonal relationships. These quotes emphasize the value of understanding and managing our own emotions, as well as empathizing with and connecting to others on a deeper level, which contributes to a more fulfilling life.

"Don't take anything personally, ... nothing other people do is because of you. It is because of themselves."

   – Don Miguel Ruiz, The Four Agreements

# Self-Discovery

"Where there's anger, there is always pain underneath."
- Eckhart Tolle

"Freedom is what you do with what's been done to you."
- Jean-Paul Sartre

"A joke is an epitaph for an emotion."
- Fredrich Nietzsche

"There's only one thing more contagious than a good attitude – a bad one."
- John C, Maxwell, Attitude

"Attitude is a choice. Happiness is a choice. Optimism is a choice. Kindness is a choice. Giving is a choice. Respect is a choice. Whatever choice you make makes you. Choose wisely."
- Roy T. Bennett

"We can all live with doubts, it's the knowing that breaks us"
- unknown

"Knowing your own darkness is the best method for dealing with the darkness of other people."
- Carl Jung

"Two people can see the same thing, disagree, and yet both be right. It's not logical; it's psychological."
- Stephen Covey, The 7 Habits of Highly Effective People

# Self-Discovery

"People not only gain understanding through reflection, they evaluate and alter their own thinking."
    - Albert Bandura, Social Foundations of Thought and Action

"Every morning we are born again. What we do today is what matters most."
    - Buddha

"Everything that irritates us about others can lead us to an understanding of ourselves."
    - Carl Gustav Jung

"You can only find out what you actually believe (rather than what you think you believe) by watching how you act. You simply don't know what you believe, before that. You are too complex to understand yourself."
    - Jordan B. Peterson, 12 Rules for Life

"First learn the meaning of what you say, and then speak."
    - Epictetus

"Character cannot be developed in ease and quiet. Only through experience of trial and suffering can the soul be strengthened, ambition inspired, and success achieved."
    - Helen Keller

"You will never be happy if you continue to search for what happiness consists of. You will never live if you are looking for the meaning of life."
    - Albert Camus

# Self-Discovery

"Knowing yourself is the beginning of all wisdom."
    - Aristotle

"Authenticity is a collection of choices that we have to make every day. It's about the choice to show up and be real. The choice to be honest. The choice to let our true selves be seen."
    - Brené Brown

"Your relationship with yourself sets the tone for every other relationship you have."
    - Robert Holden

"Before you can truly love others, you must love and understand yourself."
    - unknown

"Always trust your instincts, for they are messages from your true self."
    - unknown

"Always remember, you are braver than you believe, stronger than you seem, and smarter than you think."
    - Christopher Robin

"The most important relationship you can have is the one with yourself. Nurture it, cherish it, and invest time in it."
    - unknown

"Learning to love yourself is the greatest love of all."
    - Michael Masser & Linda Creed

Self-Discovery

"Self-awareness is the starting point for personal growth, success, and happiness."
  – unknown

"Knowing your own darkness is the best method for dealing with the darkness of other people."
  - Carl Gustav Jung

## Personal Values

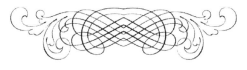

Personal values are guiding beliefs and priorities that shape one's attitudes, behaviors, and decisions, reflecting their cultural, social, and moral background. As an internal compass, these values help navigate life, assess choices, and interact with others in alignment with one's convictions. These quotes emphasize the significance of personal values in directing our thoughts and actions, reminding us to live by our core principles.

# Self-Discovery

"A person's worth in this world is estimated according to the value he places on himself."
- unknown

"Man's desires are limited by his perceptions; none can desire what he has not perceived."
- William Blake, There is no natural religion

"What the superior man seeks in himself, what the small man seeks in others."
- Confucius

"There are not perfect men in this world, only perfect intentions."
- Robin Hood: Prince of Thieves (Movie)

"Not only must we be good, but we must also be good for something."
- Henry David Thoreau

"Be the change you wish to see in the world."
- Mahatma Gandhi

"There is never a better measure of what a person is than what he becomes when he's absolutely free to choose."
- William M. Bulger

"Great minds discuss ideas; average minds discuss events; small minds discuss other people."
- Elanor Roosevelt

# Self-Discovery

"It is not in the stars to hold our destiny but in ourselves."
    - William Shakespeare

"Do not let the opinions of others define you. Do not let the limitations of others limit your vision."
    - Roy T. Bennett, The Light in the Heart

"Remember always that you not only have the right to be an individual, you have an obligation to be one."
    - Eleanor Roosevelt

"What lies before us and what lies behind us are small matters compared to what lies within us. And when we bring what is within us out into the world, miracles happen."
    - Henry David Thoreau

"Character building begins in our infancy and continues until death."
    - Eleanor Roosevelt

"Know the difference between those who stay to feed the soil and those who come to grab the fruit."
    - Suzy Kassem

"The journey of self-discovery is the most important journey of our lives."
    - Shakti Gawain

"Who we are is a result of our choices and actions. We must take responsibility for the person we have become."
    - unknown

# Self-Discovery

"Sometimes the people around you won't understand your journey. They don't need to; it's not for them."
- Joubert Botha

"The most beautiful people we have known are those who have known defeat, known suffering, known struggle, known loss, and have found their way out of the depths."
- Elisabeth Kubler-Ross

"No one can make you feel inferior without your consent."
- Eleanor Roosevelt

"Who you become is infinitely more important than what you do, or what you have."
- Zig Ziglar

"In order to be truly happy, you must live along with, and you must stand for something larger than yourself."
- Oprah Winfrey

"Your worth consists in what you are and not in what you have."
- Thomas A. Edison

"Values are like fingerprints. Nobody's are the same, but you leave them all over everything you do."
- Elvis Presley

"Happiness is that state of consciousness which proceeds from the achievement of one's values."
- Ayn Rand

Self-Discovery

"Each person's task in life is to become an increasingly better person."
    - Leo Tolstoy

"When your values are clear to you, making decisions becomes easier."
    - Roy E. Disney

"To embark on the journey of self-discovery is to uncover the values that guide your life and give it meaning."
    - unknown

"Trust the process of self-discovery. As you learn more about yourself, you will grow in ways you never thought possible."
    - unknown

"Love yourself enough to set boundaries. Your time and energy are precious. You get to choose how you use it. You teach people how to treat you by deciding what you will and won't accept."
    - Anna Taylor

"Our values are the foundation of our lives; they shape our choices, relationships, and the world around us."
    - unknown

# Mindfulness

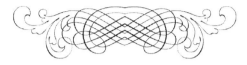

Mindfulness refers to the practice of consciously focusing on the present moment, while maintaining an attitude of non-judgment and open awareness. By cultivating mindfulness in our everyday lives, we can experience increased inner tranquility, mental clarity, and emotional resilience. The following quotes serve as an inspiration to foster mindfulness and embrace the power of being fully present in each moment.

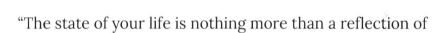

"The state of your life is nothing more than a reflection of your state of mind."
- Dr. Wayne Dyer

"Until you make the unconscious conscious, it will direct your life, and you will call it fate."
- Carl Jung

"An unexamined life is not worth living."
-Socrates

"An intellectual is someone whose mind watches itself."
- Albert Camus 1913-1960 Notebooks

## Self-Discovery

"Look at yourself with one eye, listen to yourself with the other."
- Eugene Ianesco 1912-1994 Improvisation

"The moment you become aware of the ego in you, it is strictly speaking no longer the ego, but just an old, conditioned mind-pattern. Ego implies unawareness. Awareness and ego cannot coexist."
- Eckhart Tolle

"Put your house in order to discover what you really want to do."
- Marie Kondo

"Men of superior mind busy themselves first in getting at the root of things; and when they have succeeded in this , the right course is open to them."
- Confucius

"We all have within us a center of stillness surrounded by silence."
- Dag Hammarskjöld

"He who knows others is wise; he who knows himself is enlightened."
- Lao Tzu

"The unexamined life is not worth living, but the unlived life is not worth examining."
- anonymous

# Self-Discovery

"Who looks outside, dreams; who looks inside, awakes."
    - Carl Gustav Jung

"Know thyself, for once we know ourselves, we may learn how to care for ourselves."
    - Socrates

"Self-knowledge is the beginning of self-improvement."
    - Baltasar Gracian

"Knowing others is intelligence; knowing yourself is true wisdom. Mastering others is strength; mastering yourself is true power."
    - Lao Tzu

"The greatest gift you can give to yourself is self-awareness. Know yourself and be true to your essence."
    - unknown

"Self-discovery is a journey of introspection, learning to understand our strengths and weaknesses, and finding the courage to become our best selves."
    - unknown

"The only journey is the one within."
    - Rainer Maria Rilke

"Self-awareness is the ability to take an honest look at your life without any attachment to it being right or wrong, good or bad."
    - Debbie Ford

Self-Discovery

"Self-discovery is not a destination, but a lifelong journey of exploration, understanding, and growth."
- unknown

"Discovering your true self requires honesty, vulnerability, and courage."
- unknown

"Your life is a reflection of your thoughts. If you change your thinking, you change your life."
- Brian Tracy

"Mindfulness is the aware, balanced acceptance of the present experience."
- Jon Kabat-Zinn

"The best way to capture moments is to pay attention. This is how we cultivate mindfulness."
- Jon Kabat-Zinn

"Mindfulness is simply being aware of what is happening right now without wishing it were different."
- James Baraz

"Meditation is not evasion; it is a serene encounter with reality."
- Thich Nhat Hanh

"The mind is just like a muscle - the more you exercise it, the stronger it gets and the more it can expand."
- Idowu Koyenikan

Self-Discovery

"The more emotionally intelligent you are, the more you can understand yourself and others, and the better your relationships will be."
- unknown

"In the end, just three things matter: How well we have lived, How well we have loved, How well we have learned to let go."
- Jack Kornfield

## Self-Acceptance

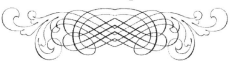

In this section, we present a collection of inspiring quotes that promote self-acceptance. Embracing self-love and learning to accept ourselves wholly, including our imperfections, is a vital component of personal development and overall mental and emotional well-being. Let these quotes act as gentle nudges, encouraging us to practice self-compassion and to celebrate the exceptional individuals we are, each with our own blend of strengths and flaws.

# Self-Discovery

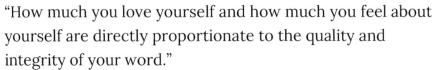

"How much you love yourself and how much you feel about yourself are directly proportionate to the quality and integrity of your word."
  - Don Miguel Ruiz, The Four Agreements

"Our love of self is so great that it becomes intolerable to let ourselves be seen in a bad light. When events threaten to cast us in a bad light, the first impulse is to throw the light off."
  - Roy Baumeister, Escaping the Self

"There is no greater agony than bearing an untold story inside you."
  - Maya Angelou

"You'll never become who you want to be if you keep blaming everyone else for who you are."
  - unknown

"There is more in us than we know. If we can be made to see it, perhaps, for the rest of our lives, we will be unwilling to settle for less."
  - Kurt Hahn

"But until a person can say deeply and honestly, "I am what I am today because of the choices I made yesterday," that person cannot say, "I choose otherwise."
  - Stephen R. Covey, The 7 Habits of Highly Effective People

## Self-Discovery

"If I'd known I was gonna live this long, I'd have taken better care of myself."
   - Eubie Blake

"You've gotta dance like there's nobody watching, Love like you'll never be hurt, Sing like there's nobody listening, And live like it's heaven on earth."
   - William W. Purkey

"One can have no smaller or greater mastery than mastery of oneself."
   - Leonardo da Vinci

"Be who you are and say what you feel, because those who mind don't matter, and those who matter don't mind."
   - Bernard M. Baruch

"Your life is a journey of learning to love yourself first and then extending that love to others in every encounter."
   - Oprah Winfrey

"Always be a first-rate version of yourself, instead of a second-rate version of somebody else."
   - Judy Garland

"Trust yourself. Create the kind of self that you will be happy to live with all your life."
   - Golda Meir

"Accept no one's definition of your life; define yourself."
   - Harvey Fierstein

## Self-Discovery

"When you know yourself, you are empowered. When you accept yourself, you are invincible."
- Tina Lifford

"Be yourself; everyone else is already taken."
- Oscar Wilde

"Be yourself. An original is always worth more than a copy."
- Suzy Kassem

"We cannot change anything till we accept it."
- Carl Jung

"Embrace the glorious mess that you are."
- Elizabeth Gilbert

"To be yourself in a world that is constantly trying to make you something else is the greatest accomplishment."
- Ralph Waldo Emerson

"Never apologize for being sensitive or emotional. Let this be a sign that you've got a big heart and aren't afraid to let others see it. Showing your emotions is a sign of strength."
- Brigitte Nicole

"The only person who can pull me down is myself, and I'm not going to let myself pull me down anymore."
- C. JoyBell C.

"Find yourself first, like yourself first, love yourself first, and friendship and love will naturally find you."
- Mandy Hale

# Self-Discovery

"Owning our story and loving ourselves through that process is the bravest thing that we will ever do."
    - Brené Brown

"I am not what happened to me, I am what I choose to become."
    - Carl Gustav Jung

"The curious paradox is that when I accept myself just as I am, then I can change."
    - Carl Rogers

"Understanding and accepting yourself is the first step to self-improvement."
    - unknown

"To be beautiful means to be yourself. You don't need to be accepted by others. You need to accept yourself."
    - Thich Nhat Hanh

"Never compromise yourself. You are all you've got."
    - Janis Joplin

"Embrace your uniqueness. Time is much too short to be living someone else's life."
    - Kobi Yamada

"Self-acceptance is the first step towards self-improvement. Love yourself for who you are and work towards becoming the best version of yourself."
    - unknown

Self-Discovery

"When we embrace who we are and decide to be authentic, instead of who we think others want us to be, we open ourselves up to real relationships, real happiness, and real success."
    - Brene Brown

"Everything that happens to you is a reflection of what you believe about yourself. We cannot outperform our level of self-esteem. We cannot draw to ourselves more than we think we are worth."
    - Iyanla Vanzant

## Facing Adversity

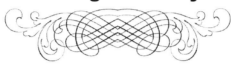

In this section, we have compiled a collection of quotes that emphasize the importance of resilience and determination when faced with adversity. These words of wisdom remind us that challenges and setbacks are inevitable in life, but it's how we confront them that defines our character and ultimately shapes our destiny.

"The winds of adversity blow away the surface issues and force us to cope with things on a deeper level."
    - Charles Stanley

"Success is to be measured not so much by the position that one has reached in life as by the obstacles which he has overcome."
    - Booker T. Washington

# Overcoming

"Never complain about the difficulties in life because a director always gives the hardest roles to his best actors."
    - unknown

"Be thankful to the bad things in life for they open your eyes to the good things you weren't paying attention to before."
    - unknown

"Out of suffering have emerged the strongest souls. The most massive characters are seared with scars."
    - Kahlil Gibran

"When a man is in despair, it means that he still believes in something."
    - Dmitri Shostakovich

"It's not what happens to us, but our response to what happens to us that hurts us."
    - Stephen R. Covey, The 7 Habits of Highly Effective People

"That which does not kill us, makes us stronger."
    - Frederich Nietzsche

"Stone walls do not a prison make, nor iron bars a cage."
    - Richard Lovelace

"When you face difficult times, know that challenges are not sent to destroy you. They're sent to promote, increase and strengthen you."
    - Joel Osteen

## Overcoming

"When I hear somebody sigh that 'life is hard', I am always tempted to ask, 'compared to what?'"
- Sidney J Harris

"Adversity has the effect of eliciting talents, which in prosperous circumstances would have lain dormant."
- Horace

"life is too short to worry about haters. They don't deserve to be an issue in your life."
- unknown

"Every adversity, every failure, every heartache carries with it the seed of an equal or greater benefit."
- Napoleon Hill

"Count your blessings not your heartaches."
- unknown

"Challenges are what make life interesting and overcoming them is what makes life meaningful."
- Joshua J. Marine

Smooth seas do not make skillful sailors."
- African Proverb

"Life is 10% what happens to us and 90% how we react to it."
- Charles R. Swindoll

"Hardships often prepare ordinary people for an extraordinary destiny."
- C.S. Lewis

Overcoming

"We don't develop courage by being happy every day. We develop it by surviving difficult times and challenging adversity."
    - Barbara De Angelis

"The greatest test of courage on earth is to bear defeat without losing heart."
    - Robert Green Ingersoll

"A smooth sea never made a skilled sailor."
    - Franklin D. Roosevelt

"Life's challenges are not supposed to paralyze you; they're supposed to help you discover who you are."
    - Bernice Johnson Reagon

"In the middle of difficulty lies opportunity."
    - Albert Einstein

"The harder you fall, the heavier your heart; the heavier your heart, the stronger you climb; the stronger you climb, the higher your pedestal."
    - Criss Jami

"It's not about how hard you can hit; it's about how hard you can get hit and keep moving forward."
    - Rocky Balboa, Rocky

"The greatest glory in living lies not in never falling, but in rising every time we fall."
    - Nelson Mandela

## Overcoming

"When you get into a tight place and everything goes against you, till it seems as though you could not hang on a minute longer, never give up then, for that is just the place and time that the tide will turn."
    - Harriet Beecher Stowe

"Sometimes you don't realize your own strength until you come face to face with your greatest weakness."
    - Susan Gale

"The ultimate measure of a man is not where he stands in moments of comfort and convenience, but where he stands at times of challenge and controversy."
    - Martin Luther King Jr.

"You never know how strong you are until being strong is your only choice."
    - Bob Marley

"Success is not built on success. It's built on failure. It's built on frustration. Sometimes it's built on catastrophe."
    - Sumner Redstone

"There is no passion to be found playing small – in settling for a life that is less than the one you are capable of living."
    - Nelson Mandela

"Your hardest times often lead to the greatest moments of your life. Keep going. Tough situations build strong people in the end."
    - Roy T. Bennett

Overcoming

"Strength does not come from winning. Your struggles develop your strengths. When you go through hardships and decide not to surrender, that is strength."
  - Arnold Schwarzenegger

## Courage & Perseverance

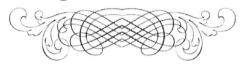

In this section, the selected quotes highlight the importance of courage and perseverance in surmounting challenges and attaining success. These insights aim to inspire you to face obstacles, overcome barriers, and unwaveringly pursue your goals. By developing resilience during adversity and embracing a growth mindset, you will be on the path to becoming a high-performance individual, positively impacting your own life and the lives of others.

"Brave doesn't mean you're not scared. It means you go on even though you're scared."
  - Angie Thomas, The Hate U Give

# Overcoming

"Fear is an illness. If you catch it and leave it untreated it can consume you." How do you treat it? "You face it."
- The Witcher S2E1

"Hope is not a strategy."
- unknown

"Courage is resistence to fear, matery of fear, not absence of fear."
- Mark Twain

"Courage doesn't always roar. Sometimes courage is the quiet voice at the end of the day saying, 'I will try again tomorrow.'"
- Mary Anne Radmacher

"You are braver than you believe, stronger than you see, and smarter than you think."
- A.A. Milne

"Every great and deep difficulty bears in itself its own solution."
- Fredrich Nietzsche

"I absorbed the loss into my life like soil receives decaying matter until it became a part of who I am."
- Jerry Sittser

"Before you embark on a journey of revenge, dig two graves."
- Confucius

# Overcoming

"Success is not the absence of failure; it's the persistence through failure."
- Aisha Tyler

"Success consists of going from failure to failure without loss of enthusiasm."
- Winston Churchill

"Our greatest glory is not in never failing, but in rising every time we fail."
- Confucius

"The harder the conflict, the more glorious the triumph."
- Thomas Paine

"The only way to discover the limits of the possible is to go beyond them into the impossible."
- Arthur C. Clarke

"Fall seven times, stand up eight."
- Japanese Proverb

"Obstacles don't have to stop you. If you run into a wall, don't turn around and give up. Figure out how to climb it, go through it, or work around it."
- Michael Jordan

"In the confrontation between the stream and the rock, the stream always wins – not through strength but by perseverance."
- H. Jackson Brown Jr.

# Overcoming

"It's not that I'm so smart, it's just that I stay with problems longer."
    - Albert Einstein

"The only limit to our realization of tomorrow will be our doubts of today."
    - Franklin D. Roosevelt

"Do not wait to strike till the iron is hot; but make it hot by striking."
    - William Butler Yeats

"Everything you've ever wanted is on the other side of fear."
    - George Addair

"The bamboo that bends is stronger than the oak that resists."
    - Japanese Proverb

"Strength doesn't come from what you can do. It comes from overcoming the things you once thought you couldn't."
    - Rikki Rogers

"When something is important enough, you do it even if the odds are not in your favor."
    - Elon Musk

"He who is not courageous enough to take risks will accomplish nothing in life."
    - Muhammad Ali

Overcoming

"It always seems impossible until it's done."
    - Nelson Mandela

## **Acceptance & Personal Growth**

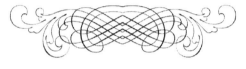

This section contains quotes that focus on the transformative power of acceptance and personal growth in overcoming life's challenges. These thought-provoking words of wisdom encourage us to embrace our experiences, learn from our mistakes, and grow into the best version of ourselves as we navigate through life's inevitable ups and downs.

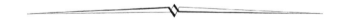

"Atonement corrects illusion not truth."
    - unknown

"We cannot change anything until we accept it. Condemnation does not liberate, it oppresses."
    - Carl Jung

# Overcoming

"We cannot solve our problems with the same thinking we used when we created them."
    - Albert Einstein

"The most terrifying thing is to accept oneself completely."
    - Carl Jung

"Some things look negative on the surface but you will soon realize that space is being created in your life for something new to emerge."
    - Eckhart Tolle

"Your mistakes do not define you."
    - unknown

"The best revenge is not to be like your enemy."
    - Marcus Aurelius

"Instead of worrying about what you cannot control, shift your energy to what you can create."
    - Roy T. Bennett

"Reject your sense of injury, and the injury itself disappears."
    - Marcus Aurelius

"Only time can heal what reason cannot."
    - Seneca

"Feelings are something you have; not something you are."
    - Shannon L. Alder

## Overcoming

"Sometimes you have to love yourself to find out who you really are."
- unknown

"Harness your mistakes, don't bow before them."
- Lisa Von Germert

"Emotion, which is suffering, ceases to be suffering as soon as we form a clear and precise picture of it."
- Spinoza

"Have you realized that most of your unhappiness in life is due to the fact that you are listening to yourself rather than talking to yourself?"
- Martin Loyd Jones

"Self-belief does not necessarily ensure success, but self-disbelief assuredly spawns failure."
- Albert Bandura, Self-efficacy: The Exercise of Control

"Our environment, the world in which we live and work, is a mirror of our attitudes and expectations."
- Earl Nightingale

"The greatest weapon against stress is our ability to choose one thought over another."
- William James

"Growth is painful. Change is painful. But nothing is as painful as staying stuck somewhere you don't belong."
- Mandy Hale

# Overcoming

"The will to win, the desire to succeed, the urge to reach your full potential... these are the keys that will unlock the door to personal excellence."
- Confucius

"We cannot become what we want by remaining what we are."
- Max DePree

"The best way to gain self-confidence is to do what you are afraid to do."
- Swati Sharma

"Don't let the past steal your present. Your past has not defined, deterred or defeated you. It has only strengthened who you are today."
- Karen Salmansohn

"Character cannot be developed in ease and quiet. Only through experience of trial and suffering can the soul be strengthened, ambition inspired, and success achieved."
- Helen Keller

"The gem cannot be polished without friction, nor man perfected without trials."
- Chinese Proverb

"The greatest discovery of any generation is that a human being can alter his life by altering his attitude."
- William James

Overcoming

"Out of difficulties grow miracles."
- Jean de la Bruyere

## **Overcoming Fear**

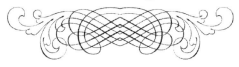

In this section, we have gathered quotes that address the topic of overcoming fear. Fear can be a beneficial powerful force, but it can also be an obstacle to growth and success. The quotes in this section provide inspiration and guidance for facing our fears head-on, embracing vulnerability, and ultimately, gaining the courage to overcome the barriers that hold us back from realizing our full potential.

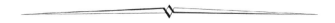

"Sometimes our deepest hate is about the things we cannot [believe we can] change in ourselves."
- The Witcher S2E5

"There is only one thing I dread: not to be worthy of my sufferings."
- Dostoevsky

# Overcoming

"Darkness cannot drive out darkness: only light can do that. Hate cannot drive out hate: only love can do that."
- Martin Luther King Jr., A Testament of Hope: The Essential Writings and Speeches

"Don't Take Anything Personally. Nothing others do is because of you. What others say and do is a projection of their own reality, their own dream. When you are immune to the opinions and actions of others, you won't be the victim of needless suffering."
- Don Miguel Ruiz

"Evil is unspectacular and always human."
-W.H. Auden

"Embrace the worst, then let go."
- anonymous

"Healers are spiritual warriors who have found the courage to defeat the darkness of their souls. Awakening and rising from the depths of their deepest fears, like a phoenix rising from the ashes, reborn with a wisdom and strength that creates a light that shines bright enough to help encourage, and inspire others out of their own darkness."
- Melanie Koulouris

"Reality has its own power – you can turn your back on it, but it will find you in the end, and your inability to cope with it will be your ruin."
- Robert Greene

# Overcoming

"The only way to overcome fear is to face it head-on and push through it."
- unknown

"Resentment is like drinking poison and then hoping it will kill your enemies."
- Nelson Mandela or Janet Parshall

"Others may hate you, but those who hate you don't win unless you hate them, and then you destroy yourself."
- Richard Nixon

"You gain strength, courage, and confidence by every experience in which you really stop to look fear in the face. You must do the thing you think you cannot do."
- Eleanor Roosevelt

"Fear is the main source of superstition, and one of the main sources of cruelty. To conquer fear is the beginning of wisdom."
- Bertrand Russell

"Inaction breeds doubt and fear. Action breeds confidence and courage. If you want to conquer fear, do not sit home and think about it. Go out and get busy."
- Dale Carnegie

"I learned that courage was not the absence of fear, but the triumph over it. The brave man is not he who does not feel afraid, but he who conquers that fear."
- Nelson Mandela

# Overcoming

"Fear is only as deep as the mind allows."
    - Japanese Proverb

"Don't carry the burden of things you don't control."
    - unknown

"The greatest mistake you can make in life is to be continually fearing you will make one."
    - Elbert Hubbard

"To escape fear, you have to go through it, not around it."
    - Richie Norton

"Fear keeps us focused on the past or worried about the future. If we can acknowledge our fear, we can realize that right now we are okay."
    - Thich Nhat Hanh

"Fears are nothing more than a state of mind."
    - Napoleon Hill

"Do the thing you fear most, and the death of fear is certain."
    - Mark Twain

"You can conquer almost any fear if you will only make up your mind to do so. For remember, fear doesn't exist anywhere except in the mind."
    - Dale Carnegie

Overcoming

## **Hopefulness**

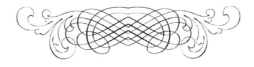

This section highlights the importance of hopefulness in overcoming life's challenges. These powerful words of wisdom remind us that, even in the darkest moments, hope can be a guiding light, offering strength, inspiration, and a renewed sense of purpose as we navigate the path toward a brighter future.

---

"Never let your hope fade. Even if you don't get what you want, believe there is a reason. Perhaps it's because better things are coming your way ... wait for it and keep the faith."
    - unknown

"You may encounter many defeats, but you must not be defeated. In fact, it may be necessary to encounter the defeats, so you can know who you are, what you can rise from, and how you can still come out of it."
    - Maya Angelou

"When you arise in the morning, think of what a precious privilege it is to be alive – to breathe, to think, to enjoy, to love."
    - Marcus Aurelius

# Overcoming

"There is a battle of two wolves inside us all, one is evil ... the other is good. The wolf that wins is the one you feed."
    - Cherokee proverb

"Good people give you happiness, bad ones give you experience, the worst ones give you lessons, the best people give you memories."
    - unknown

"Most of the important things in the world have been accomplished by people who have kept on trying when there seemed to be no hope at all."
    - Dale Carnegie

"The greater the obstacle, the more glory in overcoming it."
    - Molière

"A problem is a chance for you to do your best."
    - Duke Ellington

"Believe you can, and you're halfway there."
    - Theodore Roosevelt

"Adversity causes some men to break; others to break records."
    - William Arthur Ward

"The key to life is accepting challenges. Once someone stops doing this, they're dead."
    - Bette Davis

Overcoming

"Hope is being able to see that there is light despite all of the darkness."
- Desmond Tutu

"It is not the mountain we conquer but ourselves."
- Sir Edmund Hillary

"Once you choose hope, anything's possible."
- Christopher Reeve

"Learn from yesterday, live for today, hope for tomorrow. The important thing is not to stop questioning."
- Albert Einstein

"Everything that is done in this world is done by hope."
- Martin Luther

"There is some good in this world, and it's worth fighting for."
- J.R.R. Tolkien

"Hope is the pillar that holds up the world. Hope is the dream of a waking man."
- Pliny the Elder

"Optimism is the faith that leads to achievement. Nothing can be done without hope and confidence."
- Helen Keller

"When you're at the end of your rope, tie a knot and hold on."
- Theodore Roosevelt

"The best way to not feel hopeless is to get up and do something. Don't wait for good things to happen to you. If you go out and make some good things happen, you will fill the world with hope, you will fill yourself with hope."
   - Barack Obama

"Hope is not the conviction that something will turn out well, but the certainty that something makes sense, regardless of how it turns out."
   - Vaclav Havel

"To be without hope is like being without goals, what are you working towards?"
   - Catherine Pulsifer

"Hope is the power of being cheerful in circumstances that we know to be desperate."
   - G.K. Chesterton

"Hope begins in the dark, the stubborn hope that if you just show up and try to do the right thing, the dawn will come."
   - Anne Lamott

"Keep your face always toward the sunshine—and shadows will fall behind you."
   - Walt Whitman

"Hope is like the sun, which, as we journey toward it, casts the shadow of our burden behind us."
   - Samuel Smiles

# Overcoming

"Hope is the only thing stronger than fear."
 - Suzanne Collins

"A single thread of hope is still a very powerful thing."
 - unknown

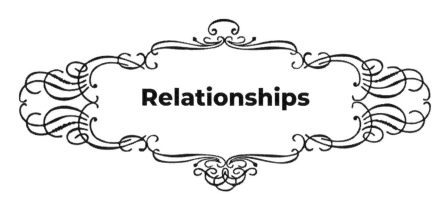

## Building Trust

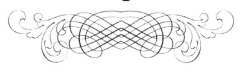

Trust is the cornerstone of every successful relationship. In this section, we explore quotes that emphasize the importance of trust, the consequences of breaking it, and how to cultivate it in our relationships. These quotes remind us that trust is earned through consistent actions and open communication, creating a strong foundation for lasting connections.

"When the trust account is high, communication is easy, instant, and effective."
    − Stephen R. Covey, The 7 Habits of Highly Effective People

"You can make more friends in two months by becoming interested in other people than you can in two years by trying to get other people interested in you."
    - Dale Carnegie

Relationships

"Don't laugh at other people, when you do, the people around you naturally wonder whether you sometimes laugh at them."
- Jeff Haden

"Trust is the glue of life. It's the most essential ingredient in effective communication. It's the foundational principle that holds all relationships."
- Stephen Covey

"You cannot control the behavior of others, but you can always choose how you respond to it."
- Roy T. Bennett, The Light in the Heart

"Trust takes years to build, seconds to break, and forever to repair."
- unknown

"The fragrance of flowers spreads only in the direction of the wind. But the goodness of a person spreads in all directions."
- unknown

"When you respect others, you respect yourself."
- John Wooden

"Friendship depends on trust, not money, not power, not mere education or knowledge. Only if there is trust will there be friendship."
- Dalai Lama

# Relationships

"Trust starts with truth and ends with truth."
    - Santosh Kalwar

"Whoever is careless with the truth in small matters cannot be trusted with important matters."
    - Albert Einstein

"The best way to find out if you can trust somebody is to trust them."
    - Ernest Hemingway

"Trust is built on actions, not words."
    - unknown

"You may be deceived if you trust too much, but you will live in torment if you don't trust enough."
    - Frank Crane

"Success in any relationship or endeavor begins with trust."
    - Stephen Covey

"Respect is earned, honesty is appreciated, trust is gained, loyalty is returned."
    - unknown

"Strong relationships are built on a foundation of trust, understanding, and mutual respect."
    - unknown

"To be trusted is a greater compliment than being loved."
    - George MacDonald

Relationships

"The only way love can last a lifetime is if it's unconditional. The truth is this: love is not determined by the one being loved but rather by the one choosing to love."
- Stephen Kendrick

"Love is the condition in which the happiness of another person is essential to your own."
- Robert A. Heinlein

"Love is when the other person's happiness is more important than your own."
- H. Jackson Brown Jr.

"The best proof of love is trust."
- Joyce Brothers

"A healthy relationship is built on unwavering trust."
- Beau Mirchoff

## Communication

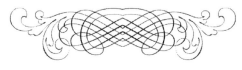

Effective communication is vital in maintaining healthy relationships. This section includes quotes that highlight the power of open and honest communication, the significance of listening, and the art of expressing oneself. These quotes encourage us to be mindful of our words and actions, fostering a deeper understanding between ourselves and others.

"Two monologues do not make a dialogue."
- Jeff Daly

"Find a group of people who challenge and inspire you, spend a lot of time with them, and it will change your life."
- Amy Poehler

"Wise men speak because they have something to say; Fools because they have to say something."
- Plato

"A friend is one of the nicest things you can have and one of the best things you can be."
- Douglas Pagels

"There is greatness in doing something you hate for the sake of someone you love."
- Shmuley Boteach

"Most people do not listen with the intent to understand; they listen with the intent to reply."
- Stephen R. Covey, The 7 Habits of Highly Effective People

# Relationships

"you can't help everyone, but everyone can help someone."
  - Ronald Regan

"Speak no evil of the absent, for it is unjust."
  - George Washington

"Don't Make Assumptions. Find the courage to ask questions and to express what you really want. Communicate with others as clearly as you can to avoid misunderstandings, sadness and drama. With just this one agreement, you can completely transform your life."
  - Don Miguel Ruiz, The Four Agreements

"Sometimes our light goes out. But is blown again into instant flame by an encounter with another human being."
  - Albert Schweitzer

"The greatest communication skill is paying value to others."
  - Denis Waitley

"To listen well is as powerful a means of communication and influence as to talk well."
  - John Marshall

"The most important thing in communication is hearing what isn't being said."
  - Peter Drucker

"Listen with curiosity. Speak with honesty. Act with integrity."
  - Roy T. Bennett

# Relationships

"Silence is often misinterpreted, but never misquoted."
- Nancy Gibbs

"The greatest compliment that was ever paid me was when someone asked me what I thought, and attended to my answer."
- Henry David Thoreau

"To handle yourself, use your head; to handle others, use your heart."
- Eleanor Roosevelt

"In the end, we will remember not the words of our enemies, but the silence of our friends."
- Martin Luther King Jr.

"One of the most sincere forms of respect is actually listening to what another has to say."
- Bryant H. McGill

"Listen with curiosity. Speak with honesty. Act with integrity."
- Roy T. Bennett

"Love does not consist in gazing at each other, but in looking outward together in the same direction."
- Antoine de Saint-Exupéry

"An eye for an eye will only make the whole world blind."
- Mahatma Gandhi

Relationships

"The language of friendship is not words but meanings."
- Henry David Thoreau

"Love is not only something you feel, it is something you do."
- David Wilkerson

"Love looks not with the eyes, but with the mind, and therefore is winged Cupid painted blind."
- William Shakespeare

## **Support and Encouragement**

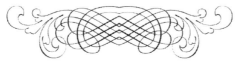

In this section, we delve into quotes that emphasize the value of supporting and encouraging our loved ones in their pursuits. These quotes inspire us to be there for each other through thick and thin, lifting each other up during challenging times and celebrating each other's successes. Support and encouragement create a nurturing environment for personal growth and the strengthening of relationships.

# Relationships

"True friendship comes when the silence between two people is comfortable."
    - David Tyson

"We can improve our relationships with others by leaps and bounds if we become encouragers instead of critics."
    - Joyce Meyer

"The best way to find yourself is to lose yourself in the service of others."
    - Mahatma Gandhi

"Be genuinely interested in everyone you meet and everyone you meet will be genuinely interested in you."
    - Rasheed Ogunlaru

"Be slow to fall into friendship, but when you are in, continue firm and constant."
    - Socrates

"Surround yourself with only people who are going to lift you higher."
    - Oprah Winfrey

"In the end, the love you take is equal to the love you make."
    - Paul McCartney

"Encourage and support your kids because children are apt to live up to what you believe of them."
    - Lady Bird Johnson

# Relationships

"Sometimes being a friend means mastering the art of timing. There is a time for silence. A time to let go and allow people to hurl themselves into their own destiny. And a time to prepare to pick up the pieces when it's all over."
- Gloria Naylor

"Never look down on anybody unless you're helping them up."
- Jesse Jackson

"Love is not about how much you say 'I love you,' but how much you prove that it's true."
- unknown

"The most important ingredient we put into any relationship is not what we say or what we do, but what we are."
- Stephen Covey

"A word of encouragement during a failure is worth more than an hour of praise after success."
- unknown

"None of us, including me, ever do great things. But we can all do small things, with great love, and together we can do something wonderful."
- Mother Teresa

"A loyal friend laughs at your jokes when they're not so good and sympathizes with your problems when they're not so bad."
- Arnold H. Glasow

# Relationships

"In relationships, the little things are the big things."
 - Stephen Covey

"A true friend never gets in your way unless you happen to be going down."
 - Arnold H. Glasow

"A real friend is one who walks in when the rest of the world walks out."
 - Walter Winchell

"The greatest gift you can give someone is your time, your attention, your love, your concern."
 - Joel Osteen

"Friendship improves happiness and abates misery, by the doubling of our joy and the dividing of our grief."
 - Marcus Tullius Cicero

"Be an encourager. The world has plenty of critics already."
 - Dave Willis

"We rise by lifting others."
 - Robert Ingersoll

"The best way to cheer yourself up is to try to cheer somebody else up."
 - Mark Twain

Relationships

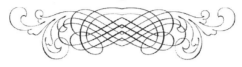

## Resolving Conflict

Conflicts are an inevitable part of any relationship. This section features quotes that offer insight into resolving conflicts in a healthy, constructive manner, emphasizing empathy, understanding, and effective communication. These quotes remind us that conflicts can lead to personal growth and relationship development if approached with an open mind and a willingness to learn.

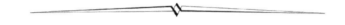

"Forgiveness liberates the soul, it removes fear. That's why it's such a powerful weapon."
- Nelson Mandela

"He that cannot forgive others breaks the bridge over which he himself must pass."
- George Herbert

"Knowing yourself is the beginning of all wisdom."
- Aristotle

"The most basic of all human needs is the need to understand and be understood. The best way to understand people is to listen to them."
- Ralph G. Nichols

## Relationships

"For lack of wood the fire dies out; and when there is no tale bearer, strife subsides."
    - Proverbs 26:20

"You do not have to attend every argument you are invited to"
    - Mandy Hale

"The more we can hear what people are feeling and needing rather than what they are thinking, the more easily we will find our way to harmony."
    - Marshall B. Rosenberg

"When we understand the needs that motivate our own and others' behavior, we have no enemies."
    - Marshall B. Rosenberg

"Sometimes you have to let go of old habits and patterns to make space for new and healthier ones."
    - Karen Salmansohn

"It takes a strong heart to love but it takes a stronger heart to love after being hurt."
    - unknown

"Do not let the behavior of others destroy your inner peace."
    - Dalai Lama

"The more we empathize with the other party, the safer we feel."
    - Marshall B. Rosenberg

Relationships

"Apologizing does not always mean you're wrong and the other person is right. It just means you value your relationship more than your ego."
  - unknown

"True humility is not thinking less of yourself; it is thinking of yourself less."
  - C.S. Lewis

"Love is an act of endless forgiveness, a tender look which becomes a habit."
  - Peter Ustinov

"Empathy is seeing with the eyes of another, listening with the ears of another, and feeling with the heart of another."
  - Alfred Adler

"Every criticism, judgment, diagnosis, and expression of anger is the tragic expression of an unmet need."
  - Marshall B. Rosenberg

"The greatest test of courage on earth is to bear defeat without losing heart."
  - Robert Green Ingersoll

"When you have a conflict, that means that there are truths that have to be addressed on each side of the conflict. And when you have a conflict, then it's an educational process to try to resolve the conflict."
  - Dolores Huerta

Relationships

"The only way out of the labyrinth of suffering is to forgive."
   - John Green

"The most important trip you may take in life is meeting people halfway."
   - Henry Boye

"Peace is not the absence of conflict, it is the ability to handle conflict by peaceful means."
   - Ronald Reagan

"When dealing with people, remember you are not dealing with creatures of logic, but with creatures bristling with prejudice and motivated by pride and vanity."
   - Dale Carnegie

## Appreciation and Gratitude

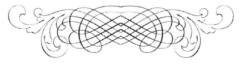

In this section, we explore quotes that highlight the importance of showing appreciation and gratitude in our relationships. These quotes inspire us to express our thankfulness for the people in our lives, acknowledging the

Relationships

positive impact they have on our well-being. Practicing gratitude strengthens the bonds we share with our loved ones, leading to happier and more fulfilling relationships.

"Your task is not to seek for love, but merely to seek and find all the barriers within yourself that you have built against it."
    - Rumi

"We accept the love we think we deserve."
    - Stephen Chbosky, The Perks of Being a Wallflower

"The purpose of a relationship is not to have another who might complete you, but to have another with whom you might share your completeness."
    - Neale Donald Walsh

"I have learned silence for the talkative, tolerance from the intolerant, kindness from the unkind. Yet strange, I am ungrateful to these teachers."
    - Kahlil Gibran

"The ache for home lives in all of us. The place where we can go as we are and not be questions."
    - Maya Angelou

"I finally learned what life is all about, it's hanging on when your heart has had enough, and giving more when you wanna give up."
    - unknown

"We are never so defenseless against suffering as when we love."
  - Sigmund Freud

"Keep love in your heart, a life without it is like a sunless garden when the flowers are dead."
  - Oscar Wilde

"I wish friends were like money, so you can hold them up to the light to see which one is real from which is fake."
  - unknown

"True friends are those who care without hesitation, remember without limitation, and forgive without explanation"
  - unknown

"If a woman is feeling cherished, she will respect a man (and vice versa)"
  - unknown

"The greatest gift of life is friendship, and I have received it."
  - Hubert H. Humphrey

"The only way to have a friend is to be one."
  - Ralph Waldo Emerson

"Learn to appreciate the people who want to be in your life and stop stressing over people who don't want to be in your life."
  - unknown

Relationships

"Love is the only force capable of transforming an enemy into a friend."
- Martin Luther King Jr.

"True friendship isn't about being inseparable, it's being separated and nothing changes."
- unknown

"Life becomes easier and more beautiful when we can see the good in other people."
- Roy T. Bennett

"A true friend is someone who thinks that you are a good egg even though he knows that you are slightly cracked."
- Bernard Meltzer

"Shared joy is a double joy; shared sorrow is half a sorrow."
- Swedish Proverb

"The best thing to hold onto in life is each other."
- Audrey Hepburn

"You don't love someone for their looks, or their clothes, or for their fancy car, but because they sing a song only you can hear."
- Oscar Wilde

"Connection is the energy that is created between people when they feel seen, heard, and valued; when they can give and receive without judgment."
- Brené Brown

"Kindness is a language which the deaf can hear and the blind can see."
   - Mark Twain

"Compassion and tolerance are not a sign of weakness, but a sign of strength."
   - Dalai Lama

"Your relationships will either make you or break you, and there is no such thing as a neutral relationship."
   - John C. Maxwell

"In the sweetness of friendship, let there be laughter and sharing of pleasures. For in the dew of little things, the heart finds its morning and is refreshed."
   - Kahlil Gibran

"We can improve our relationships with others by leaps and bounds if we become encouragers instead of critics."
   - Joyce Meyer

"No road is long with good company."
   - Turkish Proverb

"True love stories never have endings."
   - Richard Bach

"The best and most beautiful things in the world cannot be seen or even touched - they must be felt with the heart."
   - Helen Keller

Relationships

"The quality of your life is the quality of your relationships."
        - Anthony Robbins

## **Character, Empathy, and Love**

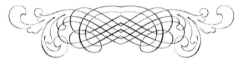

This final section includes quotes that delve into the essence of character, empathy, and love in relationships. These quotes remind us that to truly connect with others, we must first understand and accept ourselves. They also emphasize the power of empathy in fostering compassion and deep connections with others. Love, in all its forms, ties these qualities together, creating strong, resilient relationships that can stand the test of time.

"I've learned that people will forget what you said, people will forget what you did, but people will never forget how you made them feel."
        - Maya Angelou

# Relationships

"Be more concerned with your character than your reputation, because your character is what you really are, while your reputation is merely what others think you are."
  - John Wooden

"Kindness in words creates confidence. Kindness in thinking creates profoundness. Kindness in giving creates love."
  - Lao Tzu

"Everyone you meet is afraid of something, loves something, or has lost something,"
  - H. Jackson Brown Jr.

"Associate yourself with people of good quality, for it is better to be alone than in bad company."
  - Booker T. Washington

"Sometimes you will never know the value of a moment until it becomes a memory."
  - attributed to Dr. Seuss

"Treat people as if they were what they ought to be, and you help them to become what they are capable of being."
  - Johann Wolfgang von Goethe

"We don't see things as they are, we see them as we are."
  - Anaïs Nin

"Never underestimate the power of a kind word or deed."
  - unknown

Relationships

"Character is how you treat those who can do nothing for you."
    - Malcolm S. Forbes

"The true measure of a man is how he treats someone who can do him absolutely no good."
    - Samuel Johnson

"Empathy is seeing with the eyes of another, listening with the ears of another, and feeling with the heart of another."
    - Alfred Adler

"Don't let yesterday take up too much of today."
    - Will Rogers

"The only way to do great work is to love what you do."
    - Steve Jobs

"Show respect even to people who don't deserve it; not as a reflection of their character, but as a reflection of yours."
    - Dave Willis

"Never underestimate the power of a kind word or deed."
    - unknown

"Be slow to fall into friendship, but when you are in, continue firm and constant."
    - Socrates

"It's not what you have in your life, but who you have in your life that counts."
    - J.M. Laurence

# Relationships

"A loving heart is the truest wisdom."
- Charles Dickens

"Love recognizes no barriers. It jumps hurdles, leaps fences, penetrates walls to arrive at its destination full of hope."
- Maya Angelou

"The greatest thing you'll ever learn is just to love and be loved in return."
- Eden Ahbez

"A friend is someone who knows all about you and still loves you."
- Elbert Hubbard

"In the end, who among us does not choose to be a little less right to be a little less lonely?"
- Robert Brault

"You don't develop courage by being happy in your relationships every day. You develop it by surviving difficult times and challenging adversity."
- Epicurus

"Relationships are like glass. Sometimes it's better to leave them broken than to hurt yourself trying to put it back together."
- unknown

"To love and be loved is to feel the sun from both sides."
- David Viscott

Relationships

"We are born in relationship, we are wounded in relationship, and we can be healed in relationship."
- Harville Hendrix

"It's not about how many friends you have, but the quality of the friendships you have."
- Aristotle

"The greatest healing therapy is friendship and love."
- Hubert H. Humphrey

"To be yourself in a world that is constantly trying to make you something else is the greatest accomplishment."
- Ralph Waldo Emerson

"The only thing we never get enough of is love, and the only thing we never give enough of is love."
- Henry Miller

"Love is not a matter of counting the years, but making the years count."
- Michelle Amand

"Friendship is born at that moment when one person says to another, 'What! You too? I thought I was the only one.'"
- C.S. Lewis

"There's one sad truth in life I've found while journeying east and west: The only folks we really wound are those we love the best."
- Ella Wheeler Wilcox

# Relationships

"The most beautiful discovery true friends make is that they can grow separately without growing apart."
    - Elisabeth Foley

"Love is like the wind, you can't see it but you can feel it."
    - Nicholas Sparks

"Each friend represents a world in us, a world possibly not born until they arrive, and it is only by this meeting that a new world is born."
    - Anaïs Nin

"Friendship is a plant of slow growth and must undergo and withstand the shocks of adversity before it is entitled to the appellation."
    - George Washington

"Friendship multiplies the good of life and divides the evil."
    - Baltasar Gracian

"Love is not about how much you say 'I love you,' but how much you can prove that it's true."
    - unknown

"Being deeply loved by someone gives you strength, while loving someone deeply gives you courage."
    - Lao Tzu

"Love and compassion are necessities, not luxuries. Without them, humanity cannot survive."
    - Dalai Lama

# Relationships

"A loving heart is the truest wisdom."
- Charles Dickens

"Friends are the family you choose."
- Jess C. Scott

"Love is that condition in which the happiness of another person is essential to your own."
- Robert A. Heinlein

"Friendship is the hardest thing in the world to explain. It's not something you learn in school. But if you haven't learned the meaning of friendship, you really haven't learned anything."
- Muhammad Ali

"A true friend is someone who thinks that you are a good egg even though he knows that you are slightly cracked."
- Bernard Meltzer

"Love doesn't make the world go 'round. Love is what makes the ride worthwhile."
- Franklin P. Jones

"Love is like a friendship caught on fire. In the beginning a flame, very pretty, often hot and fierce, but still only light and flickering. As love grows older, our hearts mature and our love becomes as coals, deep-burning and unquenchable."
- Bruce Lee

Relationships

"To love and be loved is to feel the sun from both sides."
- David Viscott

"True friends are like diamonds - bright, beautiful, valuable, and always in style."
- Nicole Richie

"Love recognizes no barriers. It jumps hurdles, leaps fences, penetrates walls to arrive at its destination full of hope."
- Maya Angelou

## Developing Good Habits

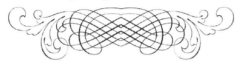

Good habits are the building blocks of a strong character and a fulfilling life. They help us make the most of our time, develop meaningful relationships, and achieve our goals. This section contains quotes that inspire and encourage the cultivation of positive habits, offering insights and guidance on how to create a life rich in purpose and fulfillment

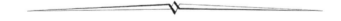

"New habits can be launched on the basis of a single, major life event, but most are built upon the foundation of many small, everyday decisions."
 - James Clear

"Replace your bad habits with good ones, and the good habits will push out the bad ones."
 - Brian Tracy

# Habits

"Start with a simple habit, and then build on it."
    - Leo Babauta

"Happiness is a habit. Cultivate it."
    - Elbert Hubbard

"If you are going to achieve excellence in big things, you develop the habits in little matters. Excellence is not an exception, it's a prevailing attitude."
    - Colin Powell

"You'll never change your life until you change something you do daily. The secret to your success is found in your daily routine."
    - John C. Maxwell

"The creation of a thousand forests is in one acorn."
    - Ralph Waldo Emmerson

"Habits are the compound interest of self-improvement."
    - James Clear, Atomic Habits

"Habit 1: Be proactive
Habit 2: Begin with the end in mind
Habit 3: Put first things first
Habit 4: Think win/win
Habit 5: Seek first to understand, then to be understood
Habit 6: Synergize
Habit 7: Sharpen the saw"
    - Stephen Covey, The 7 Habits of Highly Effective People: Powerful Lessons in Personal Change

# Habits

"Successful people are simply those with successful habits."
 - Brian Tracy

"Change might not be fast and it isn't always easy. But with time and effort, almost any habit can be reshaped."
 - Charles Duhigg, The Power of Habit

"Successful people are simply those with successful habits."
 - Brian Tracy

"Optimism is the faith that leads to achievement. Nothing can be done without hope and confidence."
 -Helen Keller

"What you stay focused on will grow."
 - Roy T. Bennett

"Action is the foundational key to all success."
 - Pablo Picasso

"If what your doing is not your passion, then you don't have anything to lose."
 - T. Harv Eker

"Every action you take is a vote for the person you wish to become."
 - James Clear, Atomic Habits

"The successful person makes a habit of doing what the failing person doesn't like to do."
 - Thomas Edison

# Habits

"Motivation is what gets you started. Habit is what keeps you going."
- Jim Rohn

"Small daily improvements are the key to staggering long-term results."
- unknown

"Habits are like financial capital – forming one today is an investment that will automatically give out returns for years to come."
- Shawn Achor

"Do something every day that brings you closer to your goals."
- unknown

"Your habits will determine your future."
- Jack Canfield

"Good habits make time your ally, bad habits make time your enemy."
- James Clear, Atomic Habits

"Success is nothing more than a few simple disciplines, practiced every day."
- Jim Rohn

"Good habits are as addictive as bad habits but much more rewarding."
- unknown

# Habits

"Choose the life that is most useful, and habit will make it the most agreeable."
    - Francis Bacon

"Good habits, which bring our lower passions and appetites under automatic control, leave our natures free to explore the larger experiences of life."
    - Ralph W. Sockman

"The best way to change a habit is to change the routine that triggers the habit."
    - James Clear

"The difference between an amateur and a professional is in their habits. An amateur has amateur habits. A professional has professional habits. We can never free ourselves from habit. But we can replace bad habits with good ones."
    - Steven Pressfield

"We are what we repeatedly do. Excellence, then, is not an act, but a habit."
    - Will Durant (summarizing Aristotle)

"Create a definite plan for carrying out your desire and begin at once, whether you are ready or not, to put this plan into action."
    - Napoleon Hill

"Forming a new habit takes 21 days. Breaking an old one takes longer."
    - Brian Tracy

"Good habits are worth being fanatical about."
- John Irving

"Every habit is driven by a craving for a change in state."
- Nir Eyal

"The easiest way to develop good habits is to start small and build upon them."
- Leo Babauta

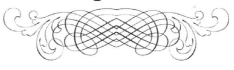

## Breaking Bad Habits

Bad habits can hold us back, hinder our growth, and have detrimental effects on our overall well-being. Recognizing and overcoming them is a vital step in personal development. In this section, you will find powerful quotes that shed light on the importance of breaking bad habits, providing wisdom and motivation to help you free yourself from their grasp and move forward with confidence.

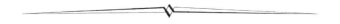

# Habits

"If you are the product (eg. social media)...It's the gradual, slight, imperceptible change in your own behavior and perception that is the product."
    - Tristan Harris, documentary "The Social Dilemma"

"Bad habits repeat themselves again and again not because you don't want to change, but because you have the wrong system for change."
    - James Clear, Atomic Habits

"The chains of habit are too weak to be felt until they are too strong to be broken."
    - Samuel Johnson

"A man who can't bear to share his habits is a man who needs to quit them."
    - Stephen King, The Dark Tower

"There are seven days in a week and someday isn't one of them."
    - Rita Chand

"A habit cannot be tossed out the window; it must be coaxed down the stairs one step at a time."
    - Mark Twain

"An unfortunate thing about this world is that the good habits are much easier to give up than the bad ones."
    - W. Somerset Maugham

# Habits

"The secret to permanently breaking any bad habit is to love something greater than the habit."
- Bryant McGill

"Without struggle, no progress and no result. Every breaking of habit produces a change in the machine."
- George Gurdjieff

"Change might not be fast and it isn't always easy. But with time and effort, almost any habit can be reshaped."
- Charles Duhigg

"Old habits will try to come back, but the key is to be aware of them and not let them take over again."
- unknown

"Old habits die hard, but with a little faith and a lot of hard work, they die before you do."
- unknown

"It is easier to prevent bad habits than to break them."
- Benjamin Franklin

"Habit, if not resisted, soon becomes necessity."
- St. Augustine

"The best way to stop a bad habit is to never begin it."
- J.C. Penney

"A nail is driven out by another nail. Habit is overcome by habit."
- Desiderius Erasmus

Habits

"Bad habits are easier to abandon today than tomorrow."
    - Yiddish Proverb

"Breaking a habit is hard, but it's a lot easier than breaking a heart."
    - anonymous

"Bad habits are like a comfortable bed, easy to get into, but hard to get out of."
    - Proverb

"The only way to truly break a bad habit is to replace it with a good one."
    - Michael Hyatt

"You leave old habits behind by starting out with the thought, 'I release the need for this in my life.'"
    - Dr. Wayne W. Dyer

"To break a bad habit, you must first understand why it exists."
    - Celestine Chua

"The first step towards getting somewhere is to decide you're not going to stay where you are."
    - J.P. Morgan

"Breaking a habit takes time and patience, but the freedom it brings is worth the effort."
    - unknown

"Habits are formed by the repetition of particular acts. They are strengthened by an increase in the number of repeated acts. Habits are also weakened or broken, and contrary habits are formed by the repetition of contrary acts."
- Mortimer J. Adler

"Breaking a bad habit is like cracking a whip; it takes a quick, firm action to get the desired result."
- Richard Branson

"The only way to break a bad habit was to replace it with a better habit."
- Jack Nicholson

"To break a bad habit, find out how it serves you, and find a new way to get the same benefit without the costs."
- Tony Robbins

"First we form habits, then they form us. Conquer your bad habits, or they will conquer you."
- Rob Gilbert

"A bad habit can be quickly broken by realizing the consequences and choosing to make a change."
- William James

Habits

## Discipline & Consistency

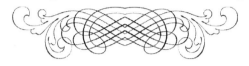

Developing and maintaining good habits requires discipline and consistency. This section features quotes that emphasize the importance of commitment and perseverance in creating lasting change. These quotes serve as a reminder that the key to success in any endeavor lies in our ability to stay disciplined and maintain consistency in our actions.

---

"Don't judge each day by the harvest you reap, but by the seeds that you plant."
- Robert Louis Stevenson

"Great things are not done by impulse, but by a series of small things brought together."
- Vincent van Gogh

"Difficult things take a long time, the impossible takes a little longer."
- Charles F. Kettering

"It always seems impossible till it's done."
- Nelson Mandela

"Goals are dreams with deadlines."
- Diana Sharf Hunt

"You can't have a plan for your day till you have a plan for your life."
- Anthony Robbins

"You do not rise to the level of your goals, you fall to the level of your systems [of habit change]."
- James Clear, Atomic Habits

"Always do your best, what you plant now, you shall harvest later."
- Og Mandino

"There's a difference between motion and action. Writing an article, that's action. Reading books on the topic, that's motion. Motion makes us feel like we are making progress without running the risk of failure."
- James Clear, Atomic Habits

"First we make our habits, then our habits make us."
- Charles C. Noble

"Even if you are on the right track, you will get run over if you just stand there."
- Will Rogers

"Success is the sum of small efforts repeated day in and day out."
- Robert Collier

# Habits

"Practice isn't the thing you do once you're good. It's the thing you do that makes you good."
  - Malcolm Gladwell

"The secret of your future is hidden in your daily routine."
  - Mike Murdock

"Small shifts in your thinking, and small changes in your energy, can lead to massive alterations of your end result."
  - Kevin Michel

"Successful people aren't born that way. They become successful by establishing the habit of doing things unsuccessful people don't like to do."
  - William Makepeace Thackeray

"Consistency is the fruit of the tree of success. The more you do something effectively and with a goal in mind, the better you will get at it and the more you will feel fulfilled."
  - Dan O'Brien

"Self-discipline is the ability to make yourself do what you should do when you should do it, whether you feel like it or not."
  - Elbert Hubbard

"Repetition of the same thought or physical action develops into a habit which, repeated frequently enough, becomes an automatic reflex."
  - Norman Vincent Peale

"Excellence is an art won by training and habituation."
    - Aristotle

"Enthusiasm is the electricity of life. How do you get it? You act enthusiastic until you make it a habit."
    - Gordon Parks

## Habit & Character

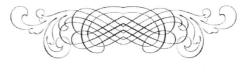

Our habits shape our character, molding us into who we are and influencing how we interact with the world around us. In this section, you'll find quotes that explore the relationship between habit and character, highlighting the profound impact our daily choices and routines have on our personal development and the people we become.

"Good people tend to teach good habits,
bad people tend to teach bad habits.
Find someone that is great and discover their habits."
    - anonymous

# Habits

"It is never too late to be what you might have been."
    - George Eliot

"All our life, so far as it has definite form, is but a mass of habits."
    - William James

"Watch your actions, they become your habits. Watch your habits, they become your character."
    – Vince Lombardi

"Your beliefs become your thoughts,
Your thoughts become your words,
Your words become your actions,
Your actions become your habits,
Your habits become your values,
Your values become your destiny."
    - Mahatma Gandhi

"Human excellence is a state of mind."
    - Socrates

"Habits change into character."
    - Ovid

"Destiny is no matter of chance, it's a matter of choice. It is not a thing to be waited for, it's a thing to be achieved."
    - William Jennings Bryan

"Character is simply habit long continued."
    - Plutarch

# Habits

"Good habits formed at youth make all the difference."
  - Aristotle

"Habits are safer than rules; you don't have to watch them. And you don't have to keep them either. They keep you."
  - Frank Crane

"Habits are like the invisible architecture of daily life. We repeat about 40% of our behavior almost daily, so our habits shape our existence and our future."
  - Gretchen Rubin

"Watch your thoughts, they become words; watch your words, they become actions; watch your actions, they become habits; watch your habits, they become character; watch your character, for it becomes your destiny."
  - often attributed to Lao Tzu

"Habit is a cable; we weave a thread of it each day, and at last we cannot break it."
  - Horace Mann

"Curious things, habits. People themselves never know they have them."
  - Agatha Christie

"Our character is basically a composite of our habits. Because they are consistent, often unconscious patterns, they constantly, daily, express our character."
  - Stephen Covey

Habits

"Sow a thought, and you reap an act;
Sow an act, and you reap a habit;
Sow a habit, and you reap a character;
Sow a character, and you reap a destiny."
    - Charles Reade

"The habits you formed early in life become your character. Live with good habits and your character will take care of itself."
    - Earl Nightingale

## Long-term Impact

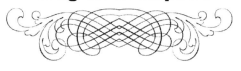

The power of habits extends beyond our immediate actions, influencing the trajectory of our lives and the legacy we leave behind. This section features quotes that reveal the long-term impact of our habits, reminding us of the importance of cultivating positive habits that will not only benefit us in the present but also shape our future and leave a lasting impression on the world.

# Habits

"Excellence is an art won by training and habituation. We do not act rightly because we have virtue or excellence, but rather have those because we have acted rightly. We are what we repeatedly do. Excellence, then, is not an act but a habit."
- Aristotle

"How we spend our day is, of course, how we spend our lives."
- Annie Dillard

"The quality of a person's life is in direct proportion to their commitment to excellence, regardless of their chosen field of endeavor."
- Vince Lombardi

"If you would plant for days, plant flowers.
If you would plant for years, plant trees.
If you would plant for eternity, plant ideas."
- proverb

"We can make ourselves miserable or make ourselves strong, the work is the same,"
- unknown

"Champions don't do extraordinary things, they do ordinary things, but they do them without thinking."
- Tony Dungy

# Habits

"All men who have turned out worth anything have had a chief hand in their own education."
- Sir Walter Scott

"Opportunity may knock once but temptation bangs on your door forever."
- Robert Fulghum

"Giving up on your goal because of a set back is like slashing your other three tires because you got a flat."
- Zig Ziglar

"I'm not afraid of failure. I feel like being afraid of failure is being afraid of success. It's the same thing."
- Kumail Nanjiani

"Quality is not an act, it is a habit."
- Will Durant (summarizing Aristotle)

"The only way to escape the personal corruption of praise is to go on working. One is tempted to stop and listen to it. The only thing is to turn away and go on working. Work is the only thing."
- Albert Einstein

"He who has a why to live for, can bear almost any how."
- Fredrich Nietzsche

"Success is the natural consequence of consistently applying the basic fundamentals."
- Jim Rohn

"The difference between an amateur and a professional is in their habits. An amateur has amateur habits. A professional has professional habits."
— Steven Pressfield

"Compound interest is the eighth wonder of the world. He who understands it earns it; he who doesn't pay it. The same principle applies to habits."
— unknown

"The only way to permanently change the temperature in the room is to reset the thermostat. In the same way, the only way to change your level of financial success 'permanently' is to reset your financial thermostat. But it is your choice whether you choose to change."
— T. Harv Eker

"Once you learn to quit, it becomes a habit."
— Vince Lombardi

"Old habits die hard, but just visualize what will happen if you give up on them."
— unknown

"Great changes may not happen right away, but with effort even the difficult may become easy."
— Bill Blackman

"It's not about breaking bad habits; it's about replacing them with good ones."
— Darren Hardy

# Habits

"Whatever I have tried to do in life, I have tried with all my heart to do it well; whatever I have devoted myself to, I have devoted myself to completely."
    - Charles Dickens

"Your net worth to the world is usually determined by what remains after your bad habits are subtracted from your good ones."
    - Benjamin Franklin

"If something can't hurt me, then why should it scare me?"
    - Jia Jiang, Rejection Proof: How I Beat Fear and Became Invincible Through 100 Days of Rejection

"Small daily improvements over time lead to stunning results."
    - Robin Sharma

"Forming good habits takes time and patience, but the benefits will last a lifetime."
    - unknown

"The power of habit is stronger than the power of reason."
    - Horace Mann

"Good habits happen when planned; bad habits happen on their own."
    - unknown

"Great is the power of habit. It teaches us to bear fatigue and to despise wounds and pain."
    - Marcus Tullius Cicero

Habits

"The easier it is to do, the harder it is to change."
    - Eng's Principle

"Good habits, once established, are just as hard to break as bad habits."
    - Robert Puller

"It's not what we do once in a while that shapes our lives, but what we do consistently."
    - Tony Robbins

"Your life does not get better by chance; it gets better by change."
    - Jim Rohn

# Leadership

## Inspiring Others

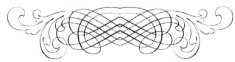

In this subsection, we explore the power of inspiration in leadership. A true leader has the ability to evoke passion and enthusiasm in others, guiding them to achieve their full potential. The quotes in this section highlight the importance of inspiring individuals to believe in themselves and strive for greatness.

"Your number one mission as a speaker is to take something that matters deeply to you and rebuild it inside the minds of your listeners."
- Chris Anderson, TED Talks

"Be the kind of leader you would follow."
- unknown

# Leadership

"It's only after you've stepped outside your comfort zone that you begin to change, grow, and transform."
- Roy T. Bennett, The Light in the Heart

"I have a dream that my four little children will one day live in a nation where they will not be judged by the color of their skin, but by the content of their character."
- Martin Luther King Jr.

"A small body of determined spirits fired by an unquenchable faith in their mission can alter the course of history."
- Mahatma Gandhi

"Treat a man as he is, and he will remain as he is;
treat a man as he can and should be,
and he will become as he can and should be."
- Goethe

"A hero is an ordinary individual who finds the strength to persevere and endure in spite of overwhelming obstacles."
- Christopher Reeve

"How wonderful it is that nobody need wait a single moment before starting to improve the world."
- Anne Frank

"Everyone can rise above their circumstances and achieve success if they are dedicated and passionate about what they do."
- Nelson Mandela

# Leadership

"People who are crazy enough to think they can change the world are the ones who can."
- Steve Jobs

"Outstanding leaders go out of their way to boost the self-esteem of their personnel. If people believe in themselves, it's amazing what they can accomplish."
- Sam Walton

"Great leaders harness personal courage, capture the hearts and minds of others, and empower new leaders to make the world a better place."
- Maxine Driscoll

"Remember that the best leaders inspire others to be the best they can be, not just do the best they can do."
- unknown

"The task of leadership is not to put greatness into people, but to elicit it, for the greatness is there already."
- John Buchan

"Treat a man as he is and he will remain as he is. Treat a man as he can and should be and he will become as he can and should be."
- Johann Wolfgang von Goethe

"A good leader inspires people to have confidence in the leader; a great leader inspires people to have confidence in themselves."
- Eleanor Roosevelt

# Leadership

"Always be a first-rate version of yourself, instead of a second-rate version of somebody else."
    - Judy Garland

"To be a great leader, you must first become a great person."
    - Robin Sharma

"Leadership is lifting a person's vision to high sights, the raising of a person's performance to a higher standard, the building of a personality beyond its normal limitations."
    - Peter Drucker

"Great leaders don't set out to be a leader. They set out to make a difference."
    - Jeremy Bravo

"To handle yourself, use your head; to handle others, use your heart."
    - Eleanor Roosevelt

"Treat a man as he is and he will remain as he is. Treat a man as he can and should be and he will become as he can and should be."
    - Johann Wolfgang von Goethe

Leadership

## **Vision & Strategy**

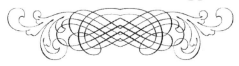

Vision and strategy are the cornerstones of effective leadership. This subsection is dedicated to the forward-thinking and planning aspects of leadership. The quotes presented here emphasize the significance of creating a compelling vision and devising a clear strategy to turn dreams into reality.

---

"All that is necessary for the triumph of evil is that good men do nothing."
    - attributed to Edmund Burke

"Victory favors those who make many calculations; defeat is often the result of too few."
    - Inspired by Sun Tzu

"Great spirits have always encountered violent opposition from mediocre minds. The mediocre mind is incapable of understanding the man who refuses to bow blindly to conventional prejudices and chooses instead to express his opinions courageously and honestly."
    - Albert Einstein

# Leadership

"The most dangerous leadership myth is that leaders are born—that there is a genetic factor to leadership. That's nonsense; in fact, the opposite is true. Leaders are made rather than born."
- Warren Bennis

"Avoid the crowd, do your own thinking, independently. Be the chess player, not the chess piece."
- unknown

"Always do what is right. It will gratify half of mankind and astound the others."
- Mark Twain

"Work like there is someone working 24 hours a day to take it away from you."
- Mark Cuban

"Leadership and learning are indispensable to each other."
- John F. Kennedy

"Good leaders create a vision, articulate the vision, passionately own the vision, and relentlessly drive it to completion."
- Jack Welch

"Where there is no vision, the people perish."
- Proverbs 29:18

"Innovation distinguishes between a leader and a follower."
- Steve Jobs

# Leadership

"The heaviest penalty for declining to rule is to be ruled by someone inferior to yourself."
    - Plato, The Republic

"Leadership is the capacity to translate vision into reality."
    - Warren Bennis

"The very essence of leadership is that you have to have a vision. It's got to be a vision you articulate clearly and forcefully on every occasion. You can't blow an uncertain trumpet."
    - Theodore Hesburgh

"Leadership is about vision and responsibility, not power."
    - Seth Berkley

"A genuine leader is not a searcher for consensus but a molder of consensus."
    - Martin Luther King, Jr.

"A leader's job is to look into the future and see the organization not as it is, but as it should be."
    - Jack Welch

"Leaders establish the vision for the future and set the strategy for getting there."
    - John P. Kotter

"A great leader's courage to fulfill his vision comes from passion, not position."
    - John C. Maxwell

# Leadership

"Leaders aren't born, they are made. And they are made just like anything else, through hard work. And that's the price we'll have to pay to achieve that goal, or any goal."
    - Vince Lombardi

"The leader has to be practical and a realist, yet must talk the language of the visionary and the idealist."
    - Eric Hoffer

"A leader is someone who demonstrates what's possible."
    - Mark Yarnell

"A visionary leader has the ability to see the potential in people, ideas, and projects, and is able to inspire others to help achieve that potential."
    - unknown

## Empowerment & Teamwork

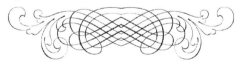

Leadership is about empowering others and fostering a collaborative environment. In this subsection, we focus on

# Leadership

the importance of nurturing teamwork and promoting a sense of shared responsibility. The quotes in this section underscore the value of empowering individuals, building trust, and fostering an environment where everyone's contribution is valued.

"Lead from the back – and let others believe they are in front."
    - Nelson Mandela

"Leadership is not about titles, positions or flowcharts. It is about one life influencing another."
    - John Maxwell

"Don't follow the crowd, let the crowd follow you."
    - Margaret Thatcher

"The [saying] is this: the more we share ... the more we have."
    - Leonard Nemoy

"You can have everything you want in life if you just help enough people get what they want in life."
    - Zig Ziglar

"A leader is one who knows the way, goes the way, and shows the way."
    - John C. Maxwell

# Leadership

"True leaders understand that leadership is not about them but about those they serve. It is not about exalting themselves but about lifting others up."
- Sheri L. Dew

"A truly rich man is one whose children run into his arms when his hands are empty."
- unknown

"No man can get rich himself unless he enriches others."
- Earl Nightengale

"Leadership is not about being in control. It's about being able to empower others."
- John C. Maxwell

"Leadership is the art of getting someone else to do something you want done because he wants to do it."
- Dwight D. Eisenhower

"Leadership is unlocking people's potential to become better."
- Bill Bradley

"Great leaders are willing to sacrifice their own personal interests for the good of the team."
- John C. Maxwell

"Great leaders find ways to connect with their people and help them fulfill their potential."
- Steven J. Stowell

# Leadership

"The greatest leader is not necessarily the one who does the greatest things. He is the one that gets the people to do the greatest things."
    - Ronald Reagan

"Before you are a leader, success is all about growing yourself. When you become a leader, success is all about growing others."
    - Jack Welch

"The best leaders are those most interested in surrounding themselves with assistants and associates smarter than they are."
    - John C. Maxwell

"Leadership is not just about giving energy. It's about unleashing other people's energy."
    - Paul Polman

"Leadership is about making others better as a result of your presence and making sure that impact lasts in your absence."
    - Sheryl Sandberg

"The greatest gift of leadership is a boss who wants you to be successful."
    - Jon Taffer

"Great things in business are never done by one person; they're done by a team of people."
    - Steve Jobs

# Leadership

"Teamwork is the ability to work together toward a common vision. The ability to direct individual accomplishments toward organizational objectives. It is the fuel that allows common people to attain uncommon results."
  - Andrew Carnegie

"None of us is as smart as all of us."
  - Ken Blanchard

"The best leaders are those who can inspire others to follow their vision while allowing them to develop their own unique paths."
  - Jeff Weiner

"To build a strong team, you must see someone else's strength as a complement to your weakness and not a threat to your position or authority."
  - Christine Caine

"The function of leadership is to produce more leaders, not more followers."
  - Ralph Nader

"The strength of the team is each individual member. The strength of each member is the team."
  - Phil Jackson

"A good leader is a person who takes a little more than his share of the blame and a little less than his share of the credit."
  - John C. Maxwell

Leadership

"A leader is best when people barely know he exists when his work is done, his aim fulfilled, they will say: we did it ourselves."
- Lao Tzu

## **Decision-making**

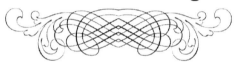

Strong decision-making skills are crucial for successful leadership. This subsection delves into the art of making effective and informed decisions, even in the face of uncertainty and challenges. The quotes presented here highlight the importance of decisiveness, courage, and the ability to weigh risks and rewards in the decision-making process.

"Management is doing things right; leadership is doing the right things."
- Peter Drucker, Essential Drucker

# Leadership

"Leadership is a potent combination of strategy and character. But if you must be without one, be without the strategy."
- Norman Schwarzkopf

"It's not your position in life, it's the disposition you have which will change your positions."
- Dr. David McKinley

"Boast not of tomorrow, for you know not what any day may bring forth."
- Proverbs 27:1

"The true test of leadership is how well you function in a crisis."
- Brian Tracy

"Be Impeccable With Your Word. Speak with integrity. Say only what you mean. Avoid using the word to speak against yourself or to gossip about others. Use the power of your word in the direction of truth and love."
- Don Miguel Ruiz

"Pray as though everything depended on God and work as though everything depended on you."
- St. Ignatius of Loyola

"Great leaders are almost always great simplifiers, who can cut through argument, debate, and doubt to offer a solution everybody can understand."
- Colin Powell

# Leadership

"The quality of a leader is reflected in the standards they set for themselves."
    - Ray Kroc

"Effective leadership is putting first things first. Effective management is discipline, carrying it out."
    - Stephen Covey

"In any moment of decision, the best thing you can do is the right thing, the next best thing is the wrong thing, and the worst thing you can do is nothing."
    - Theodore Roosevelt

"Don't be afraid to give up the good to go for the great."
    - John D. Rockefeller

"Good decision-making is a vital part of good leadership. You have to know when to break with the past and when to embrace it."
    - John C. Maxwell

"When you have to make a choice and don't make it, that is in itself a choice."
    - William James

"Leadership is solving problems. The day soldiers stop bringing you their problems is the day you have stopped leading them. They have either lost confidence that you can help or concluded you do not care. Either case is a failure of leadership."
    - Colin Powell

# Leadership

"A wise man makes his own decisions, an ignorant man follows the public opinion."
    - Grantland Rice

"The best leaders make decisions, not because they have all the information, but because they have the courage to act in the face of uncertainty."
    - Simon Sinek

"Effective leadership is not about making speeches or being liked; leadership is defined by results, not attributes."
    - Peter Drucker

"The challenge of leadership is to make those judgments. You have to be decisive. You can't sit on your hands and wring them and agonize over decisions. You have to make them and move on."
    - Carly Fiorina

"The mark of a great leader is the ability to make the hard decisions and stand by them, even in the face of adversity."
    - unknown

"You can't make decisions based on fear and the possibility of what might happen."
    - Michelle Obama

"The greatest leaders are those who can make tough decisions, even when they don't have all the answers."
    - John C. Maxwell

# Leadership

"To be a good leader, you sometimes need to go down the untraveled path. Being bold in the face of uncertainty will help give your team courage and motivate them to keep striving when the going gets tough."
 - Richard Branson

"Analyze your mistakes. You've already paid the tuition, you might as well get the lesson."
 - Tim Fargo

"It's not hard to make decisions when you know what your values are."
 - Roy Disney

"Decisiveness is a characteristic of high-performing men and women. Almost any decision is better than no decision at all."
 - Brian Tracy

"Indecision is the thief of opportunity."
 - Jim Rohn

"Every decision you make, either moves you closer to or further away from your goals."
 - John Assaraf

"Be decisive. Right or wrong, make a decision. The road of life is paved with flat squirrels who couldn't make a decision."
 - unknown

"In the end, all business operations can be reduced to three words: people, product, and profits. Unless you've got a good team, you can't do much with the other two."
    - Lee Iacocca

## Leading by Example

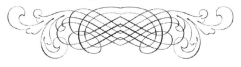

Leading by example is a fundamental aspect of leadership. In this subsection, we emphasize the importance of leaders who embody the values, principles, and behaviors they expect from others. The quotes in this section showcase the significance of being a role model and setting the standard for others to follow.

---

"Do not judge me by my successes, judge me by how many times I fell down and got back up again."
    - Nelson Mandela

# Leadership

"The greatest leader is not the one who does the greatest things. He is the one that gets the people to do the greatest things."
- Ronald Reagan

"You don't have to hold a position in order to be a leader."
- Anthony J. D'Angelo

"Real leaders must be ready to sacrifice all for the freedom of their people."
- Nelson Mandela

"Do not wait for leaders; do it alone, person to person."
- Mother Teresa

"A great man is always willing to be little."
- Ralph Waldo Emmerson

"We may encounter many defeats but we must not be defeated."
- Maya Angelou

"He is rich or poor according to what he is, not according to what he has."
- Henry Ward Beecher

"One thing you can give and still keep is your word."
- unknown

"Don't ask yourself what the world needs, ask yourself what makes you come alive, and then go do that."
- Howard Thurmon

# Leadership

"The best executive is the one who has sense enough to pick good men to do what he wants done, and self-restraint enough to keep from meddling with them while they do it."
    - Theodore Roosevelt

"A true leader has the confidence to stand alone, the courage to make tough decisions, and the compassion to listen to the needs of others."
    - Douglas MacArthur

"Leadership is an action, not a position."
    - Donald McGannon

"A true leader is someone who is humble enough to admit their mistakes and wise enough to learn from them."
    - unknown

"Leadership is not a popularity contest; it's about leaving your ego at the door. The name of the game is to lead without a title."
    - Robin Sharma

"People ask the difference between a leader and a boss. The leader leads, and the boss drives."
    - Theodore Roosevelt

"True leadership is about striving to become better in all areas of life and empowering everyone around you to become the best versions of themselves."
    - John Quincy Adams

Leadership

"Your position never gives you the right to command. It only imposes on you the duty of so living your life that others can receive your orders without being humiliated."
    - Dag Hammarskjöld

## Dealing with Opposition

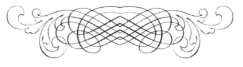

As a leader, facing opposition and challenges is part of the journey. This section delves into the resilience required to overcome difficulties and stay focused on your vision. Here, the selected quotes highlight the importance of handling criticism, resolving disputes, and remaining steadfast amidst adversity.

"Never doubt that a small group of thoughtful, concerned citizens can change the world. Indeed it is the only thing that ever has."
    - Margaret Mead

# Leadership

"No amount of evidence will ever persuade an idiot."
    - Mark Twain attributed

"As one approaches elder's status, one ceases to indulge in battles."
    - Youruba proverb

"Peace cannot be kept by force, it can only be achieved by understanding."
    - Albert Einstein

"If you want to make enemies, try to change something."
    - Woodrow Wilson

"The key to successful leadership today is influence, not authority."
    - Ken Blanchard

"Leadership is the art of giving people a platform for spreading ideas that work."
    - Seth Godin

"The challenge of leadership is to be strong but not rude; be kind, but not weak; be bold, but not a bully; be humble, but not timid; be proud, but not arrogant; have humor, but without folly."
    - Jim Rohn

"Leaders think and talk about the solutions. Followers think and talk about the problems."
    - Brian Tracy

# Leadership

"Leadership is the ability to guide others without force into a direction or decision that leaves them still feeling empowered and accomplished."
- Lisa Cash Hanson

"Stand up for what you believe in, even if it means standing alone. The strength of a true leader is the ability to withstand opposition."
- Andy Biersack

"A leader takes people where they want to go. A great leader takes people where they don't necessarily want to go, but ought to be."
- Rosalynn Carter

"Do what you feel in your heart to be right, for you'll be criticized anyway."
- Eleanor Roosevelt

"In the face of impossible odds, people who love this country can change it."
- Barack Obama

"Great leaders are willing to endure criticism and opposition for the sake of their cause."
- John C. Maxwell

"You have enemies? Good. That means you've stood up for something, sometime in your life."
- Winston Churchill

# Leadership

"To avoid criticism, do nothing, say nothing, and be nothing."
    - Elbert Hubbard

"The greater the opposition, the greater the opportunity for growth."
    - John C. Maxwel

"When you stand up for what you believe in, you will face opposition. But it's worth it to create a better world."
    - Lailah Gifty Akita

"Don't be afraid of opposition. Remember, a kite rises against, not with, the wind."
    - Hamilton Wright Mabie

"The real test of leadership is not how well you function in times of peace and calm, but how you handle adversity and opposition."
    - John Quincy Adams

"The true leader is one who can stand firm in the face of opposition and remain dedicated to their vision."
    - unknown

"When the winds of change blow, some people build walls and others build windmills."
    - Chinese Proverb

"You cannot change the world without facing resistance. Embrace the opposition and use it as fuel to push forward."
    - Germany Kent

Leadership

"Every great leader had to learn to embrace criticism and opposition as a part of the journey towards success."
- Robin S. Sharma

"The sign of a true leader is not avoiding confrontation but dealing with it effectively and compassionately."
- John C. Maxwell

## The Value of Education

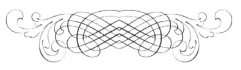

Education is a powerful tool that can transform lives and shape the world around us. In this section, you'll find quotes that highlight the importance of education and its role in personal growth, social progress, and the development of critical thinking skills. Let these words of wisdom remind you of the value of investing in education and inspire you to continue learning throughout your life.

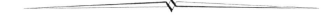

"There are two educations. One should teach us how to make a living and the other how to live."
- John Adams

"No thief, however skillful, can rob one of knowledge, and that is why knowledge is the best and safest treasure to acquire."
- L. Frank Baum, The Lost Princess of Oz

# Learning

"Education costs money, but then so does ignorance."
    - Claus Moser

"Education and slavery are incompatible with each other."
    - Frederick Douglas

"For knowledge itself is power"
    - Francis Bacon 1561-1626 Religious Meditations

"the supreme end of education is expert discernment in all things – the power to tell the good from the bad, the genuine from the counterfeit, and to prefer the good and the genuine to the bad and the counterfeit."
    - John Milton

"The ideal student values knowledge for its own sake, as well as for its instrumental uses. He or she hopes to make a contribution to society at large."
    - Carol S. Dweck, Mindset

"Education is the most powerful weapon which you can use to change the world."
    - Nelson Mandela

"Knowledge is power. Information is liberating. Education is the premise of progress, in every society, in every family."
    - Kofi Annan

"Education is the passport to the future, for tomorrow belongs to those who prepare for it today."
    - Malcolm X

# Learning

"Only the educated are free."
- Epictetus

"Knowledge will bring you the opportunity to make a difference."
- Claire Fagin

"Learning is an ornament in prosperity, a refuge in adversity, and a provision in old age."
- Aristotle

"Education is not preparation for life; education is life itself."
- John Dewey

"He who opens a school door, closes a prison."
- Victor Hugo

"Education is the ability to listen to almost anything without losing your temper or your self-confidence."
- Robert Frost

"Education is the key to unlocking the world, a passport to freedom."
- Oprah Winfrey

"The more you learn, the more you realize how little you know."
- Socrates

"Education is the movement from darkness to light."
- Allan Bloom

# Learning

"An investment in knowledge pays the best interest."
- Benjamin Franklin

"The more you know, the less you need to say."
- Jim Rohn

"Education is not the answer to the question. Education is the means to the answer to all questions."
- William Allin

"Education is not a problem. Education is an opportunity."
- Lyndon B. Johnson

"The roots of education are bitter, but the fruit is sweet."
- Aristotle

"Your education is a dress rehearsal for a life that is yours to lead."
- Nora Ephron

"Education is the kindling of a flame, not the filling of a vessel."
- Socrates

"Intelligence plus character - that is the goal of true education."
- Martin Luther King Jr.

"Education is a better safeguard of liberty than a standing army."
- Edward Everett

# Learning

"Education is the most powerful weapon which you can use to change the world."
    - Nelson Mandela

"The purpose of education is to replace an empty mind with an open one."
    - Malcolm Forbes

"Education breeds confidence. Confidence breeds hope. Hope breeds peace."
    - Confucius

"The beautiful thing about learning is that no one can take it away from you."
    - B.B. King

## Lifelong Learning

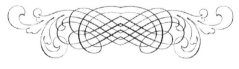

The process of learning is a never-ending journey that continues throughout our entire lives. This collection of quotes emphasizes the importance of embracing lifelong learning, as it not only enriches our minds but also shapes

# Learning

our character. Discover inspiration from these quotes to stay curious, hungry for knowledge, and committed to personal growth, no matter your age.

"The more I learn, the more I find out how little I know."
— John E. Copage

"Always walk through life as if you have something new to learn and you will."
— Vernon Howard

"Commit yourself to lifelong learning. The most valuable asset you'll ever have is your mind and what you put into it."
— Brian Tracy

"Anyone who stops learning is old, whether at twenty or eighty. Anyone who keeps learning stays young."
— Henry Ford

"Never stop learning, because life never stops teaching."
— anonymous

"Live as if you were to die tomorrow. Learn as if you were to live forever."
— Mahatma Gandhi

"I did then what I knew how to do. Now that I know better, I do better."
— Maya Angelou

# Learning

"No matter how proficient we become in something, we're still lifelong students."
    - unknown

"Develop a passion for learning. If you do, you will never cease to grow."
    - Anthony J. D'Angelo

"The purpose of learning is growth, and our minds, unlike our bodies, can continue growing as we continue to live."
    - Mortimer Adler

"Learning is a lifelong process; we can never know enough."
    - Lailah Gifty Akita

"Learning is not the product of schooling but the lifelong attempt to acquire it."
    - Albert Einstein

"It is never too late to be what you might have been."
    - George Eliot

"We should not judge people by their peak of excellence; but by the distance they have traveled from the point where they started."
    - Henry Ward Beecher

"If you are not willing to learn, no one can help you. If you are determined to learn, no one can stop you."
    - Zig Ziglar

# Learning

"Learning to learn is to know how to navigate in a forest of facts, ideas, and theories, a proliferation of constantly changing items of knowledge."
  - Raymond Quenean

"Try to learn something about everything and everything about something."
  - Thomas Huxley

"The capacity to learn is a gift; the ability to learn is a skill; the willingness to learn is a choice."
  - Brian Herbert

"Learning is like breathing; it is essential for our growth and wellbeing."
  - Debasish Mridha

"Learning is like the horizon: there is no limit."
  - Chinese Proverb

"Learning is the beginning of wealth. Learning is the beginning of health. Learning is the beginning of spirituality. Searching and learning is where the miracle process all begins."
  - Jim Rohn

"Success is no accident. It is hard work, perseverance, learning, studying, sacrifice, and most of all, love of what you are doing or learning to do."
  - Pele

# Learning

"We are not what we know but what we are willing to learn."
 - Mary Catherine Bateson

"The illiterate of the 21st century will not be those who cannot read and write, but those who cannot learn, unlearn, and relearn."
 - Alvin Toffler

"In a time of drastic change, it is the learners who inherit the future. The learned usually find themselves equipped to live in a world that no longer exists."
 - Eric Hoffer

"The more you learn, the more you earn."
 - Warren Buffett

"Wisdom is not a product of schooling but of the lifelong attempt to acquire it."
 - Albert Einstein

"Learning is not attained by chance; it must be sought for with ardor and attended to with diligence."
 - Abigail Adams

"To learn is to change. Education is a process that changes the learner."
 - George B. Leonard

"Learning is like rowing upstream, not to advance is to drop back."
 - Chinese Proverb

Learning

"The only thing better than learning from experience is learning from other people's experience."
- Warren Buffett

"The one who keeps learning is the one who will keep rising."
- Robin Sharma

"Never let formal education get in the way of your learning."
- Mark Twain

## Learning from Failure

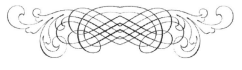

Failure is an inevitable part of life, but it can also be a powerful teacher. In this section, you'll find quotes that highlight the importance of embracing failure as an opportunity for growth and learning. Let these words of wisdom remind you that our greatest lessons often come from our setbacks and encourage you to persevere through challenges in your journey toward success.

"It's better to be uninformed than ill-informed."
- Keith Duckworth, The Search for Power

# Learning

"I was gratified to be able to answer promptly, and I did. I said I didn't know."
  - Mark Twain

"The less one knows about a world, the greater the tendency one has to apply one's beliefs and prejudices to it, be they positive or negative."
  - Christophe Guibert

"Every bit of learning is a little death. Every bit of new information challenges a previous conception, forcing it to dissolve into chaos before it can be reborn as something better. Sometimes such deaths virtually destroy us."
  - Jordan B. Peterson, 12 Rules for Life

"Mistakes are a part of being human. Appreciate your mistakes for what they are: precious life lessons that can only be learned the hard way."
  - Al Franken

"There are no secrets to success. It is the result of preparation, hard work, and learning from failure."
  - Colin Powell

"The best way to predict the future is to invent it."
  - Alan Kay

"Learning and innovation go hand in hand. The arrogance of success is to think that what you did yesterday will be sufficient for tomorrow."
  - William Pollard

# Learning

"You don't learn to walk by following rules. You learn by doing, and by falling over."
    - Richard Branson

"When we give ourselves permission to fail, we, at the same time, give ourselves permission to excel."
    - Eloise Ristad

"Education is learning what you didn't even know you didn't know."
    - Daniel J. Boorstin

"It is the mark of an educated mind to be able to entertain a thought without accepting it."
    - Aristotle

"In school, you're taught a lesson and then given a test. In life, you're given a test that teaches you a lesson."
    - Tom Bodett

"The only real mistake is the one from which we learn nothing."
    - Henry Ford

"To be conscious that you are ignorant of the facts is a great step to knowledge."
    - Benjamin Disraeli

"The only defense against the world is a thorough knowledge of it."
    - John Locke

"Mistakes are the portals of discovery."
- James Joyce

## Teaching and Mentorship

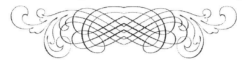

Behind every successful person is a mentor or teacher who has helped guide and inspire them. This collection of quotes celebrates the impact that teachers and mentors can have on our lives, as well as the value of sharing knowledge and experience with others. Allow these quotes to remind you of the importance of mentorship and the powerful role that teaching plays in shaping the future.

"It is the supreme art of the teacher to awaken joy in creative expression and knowledge."
- Albert Einstein

"In learning, you will teach, and in teaching, you will learn."
- Phil Collins

Learning

"He who knows not and knows not
that he knows, is a fool; show him.
He who knows not and knows that
he knows not is a child; teach him.
He who knows and knows not
that he knows is asleep; wake him.
He who knows and knows he knows
is wise; follow him."
    - Persian Proverbs

"The first sign of an educated person is that she asks more questions than she delivers answers."
    - Johnnete Cole

"I cannot teach anybody anything. I can only make them think"
    - Socrates

"Just as a piece of land has to be prepared beforehand if it is to nourish the seed, so the mind of the pupil has to be prepared in its habits if it is to enjoy and dislike the right things."
    - Aristotle

"The mediocre teacher tells. The good teacher explains. The superior teacher demonstrates. The great teacher inspires."
    - William Arthur Ward

"Self-education is the only possible education; the rest is mere veneer laid on the surface of a child's nature."
    - Charlotte Mason

# Learning

"In the end, we will conserve only what we love; we will love only what we understand and we will understand only what we are taught."
    - Baba Dioum

"If you can't explain it simply, you don't understand it well enough."
    - Albert Einstein

"Tell me and I forget, teach me and I may remember, involve me and I learn."
    - Benjamin Franklin

"The best teacher is experience and not through someone's distorted point of view."
    - Jack Kerouac

"Do not let your learning lead to knowledge. Let your learning lead to action."
    - Jim Rohn

"Learning is a process of discovery, not just remembering what someone else has taught you."
    - Ellen J. Langer

"The goal of education is not to increase the amount of knowledge but to create the possibilities for a child to invent and discover, to create men who are capable of doing new things."
    - Jean Piaget

Learning

"Teaching is only demonstrating that it is possible. Learning is making it possible for yourself."
    - Paulo Coelho

"Give a man a fish, and you feed him for a day. Teach a man to fish, and you feed him for a lifetime."
    - Chinese Proverb

"Education is not the filling of a pail but the lighting of a fire."
    - William Butler Yeats

"A teacher affects eternity; he can never tell where his influence stops."
    - Henry Adams

"Teachers can open the door, but you must enter by yourself."
    - Chinese Proverb

"He who is not a good servant will not be a good master."
    - Plato

"When one teaches, two learn."
    - Robert Heinlein

## Attaining Knowledge

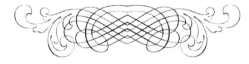

Knowledge is the foundation of personal growth and empowerment. This section features quotes that explore the relationship between knowledge and learning and the ways they can transform our lives. Find inspiration in these quotes to continue expanding your horizons, seeking new experiences, and challenging yourself to grow intellectually and emotionally.

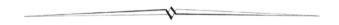

"A college education should equip one to entertain three things: a friend, an idea, and oneself."
- Thomas Ehrlich

"Measure your mind's height by the shade it casts."
- Elizabeth Barrett Browning

"It does not matter how many books you have, but how good are the books which you have."
- Seneca

"The reading of all good books is like a conversation with the finest persons of past centuries."
- Rene Descartes

# Learning

"Chance favors the prepared mind"
    - Louis Pasteur

"Man's mind, once stretched by a new idea, never regains its original dimensions."
    - Oliver Wendell Holmes

"The more you know, the more you realize you don't know."
    - Aristotle

"If you believe that no one is ever corrupted by a book, you have also to believe that no one was ever improved by a book."
    - Irving Kristol

"If I have seen farther, it is by standing on the shoulders of giants."
    - Sir Issac Newton

"The only true wisdom is in knowing you know nothing."
    - Socrates

"A library is thought in cold storage."
    - Herbert Samuel

"Reading furnishes the mind only with materials of knowledge; it is thinking that makes what we read ours."
    - John Locke

"The only person who is educated is the one who has learned how to learn and change."
    - Carl Rogers

# Learning

"Education is not the learning of facts, but the training of the mind to think."
    - Albert Einstein

"Learning never exhausts the mind."
    - Leonardo da Vinci

"Change is the end result of all true learning."
    - Leo Buscaglia

"Live as if you were to die tomorrow. Learn as if you were to live forever."
    - Mahatma Gandhi

"We learn more by looking for the answer to a question and not finding it than we do from learning the answer itself."
    - Lloyd Alexander

"Learning is a treasure that will follow its owner everywhere."
    - Chinese Proverb

"Learn everything you can, anytime you can, from anyone you can; there will always come a time when you will be grateful you did."
    - Sarah Caldwell

"The more that you read, the more things you will know. The more that you learn, the more places you'll go."
    - Dr. Seuss

# Learning

"Learning is not the product of teaching. Learning is the product of the activity of learners."
    - John Holt

"Learning is a process where knowledge is presented to us, then shaped through understanding, discussion and reflection."
    - Paulo Freire

"The mind, once stretched by a new idea, never returns to its original dimensions."
    - Ralph Waldo Emerson

"The more I read, the more I acquire, the more certain I am that I know nothing."
    - Voltaire

"True learning is not about memorizing but understanding."
    - Debasish Mridha

"Learning is not a spectator sport."
    - D. Blocher

"Learning is the only thing the mind never exhausts, never fears, and never regrets."
    - Leonardo da Vinci

"The only source of knowledge is experience."
    - Albert Einstein

"Knowledge speaks, but wisdom listens."
    - Jimi Hendrix

# Learning

"The aim of education is the knowledge, not of facts, but of values."
   - William S. Burroughs

## Curiosity and Critical Thinking

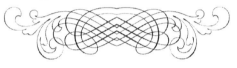

Curiosity and critical thinking are essential components of learning that allow us to engage with the world around us, ask thought-provoking questions, and challenge the status quo. This collection of quotes encourages us to embrace our innate curiosity and develop our critical thinking skills to make informed decisions, foster innovation, and deepen our understanding of the world. Allow these quotes to inspire you to think critically, ask questions, and remain curious in your pursuit of knowledge.

"Our knowledge can only be finite, while our ignorance must necessarily be infinite."
   - Karl Popper, Conjectures and Refutations

# Learning

"So that means you need to know a thing even when you don't need to know them, but because you need to know whether or not you need to know. And if you don't need to know, you still need to know sot that you know that there was no need to know,"
    - Jonathatn Lynn, Yes Prime Minister Vol II

"Any fool can know. The point is to understand."
    - Albert Einstein

"The most powerful weapon of ignorance - the diffusion of printed material."
    - Leo Tolstoy, War and Peace epilogue

"The farther backward you can look, the farther forward you are likely to see."
    - Winston Churchill

"An intellectual – one educated beyond the bounds of common sense."
    - anonymous

"The most formidable weapon against error of every kind is reason. I have never used any other and I never shall."
    - Thomas Paine

"Some beliefs truly inform you and some blind you. Some are true; some are not. But, the question is, which one is which? This kind of question – a question about quality of your beliefs – is the fundamental concern of critical thinking."
    - Lewis Vaughn, The Power Of Critical Thinking

## Learning

"The man of knowledge must be able not only to love his enemies but also to hate his friends."
    - Friedrich Nietzsche

"You only have to ask a stupid question once, if you listen to the answer."
    - Jordan Peterson

"Those who have wisdom, have no afflictions."
    - unknown

"The greatest enemy of knowledge is not ignorance, it is the illusion of knowledge."
    - Daniel J. Boorstin

"Correctness in thinking is the normal means to reach truth, which is the conformity of thought with reality."
    - Sister Miriam Joseph, Trivium

"Great minds are always feared by lesser minds."
    - Dan Brown, The Lost Symbol

"The moment you don't understand something is the moment you stop learning."
    - L. Ron Hubbard

"Ideologies are substitutes for true knowledge, and ideologues are always dangerous when they come to power, because a simple-minded I-know-it-all approach is no match for the complexity of existence."
    - Jordan B. Peterson, 12 Rules for Life

# Learning

"The art and science of asking questions is the source of all knowledge."
    - Thomas Berger

"Don't just read the easy stuff. You may be entertained by it but you will never grow from it."
    - Jim Rohn

"The sign of a maturing intellect is having the will and the courage to gradually prune beliefs that are groundless."
    - Lewis Vaughn, The Power of Critical Thinking

"Logic is useless unless it is armed with essential data."
    - unknown

"I don't want to believe, I want to know."
    - Carl Sagan

"The limits of my language means the limits of my world."
    - Ludwig Wittgenstein, Tractatus Logico-Philosophicus

"Life is a series of experiences, each one of which makes us bigger, even though sometimes it is hard to realize this. For the world was built to develop character, and we must learn that the setbacks and grieves which we endure help us in our marching onward."
    - Henry Ford

"A wise man can learn more from a foolish question than a fool can learn from a wise answer."
    - Bruce Lee

# Learning

"The important thing is not to stop questioning. Curiosity has its own reason for existing."
    - Albert Einstein

"Curiosity is the wick in the candle of learning."
    - William Arthur Ward

"The mind is not a vessel to be filled, but a fire to be kindled."
    - Plutarch

"Curiosity is the engine of achievement."
    - Sir Ken Robinson

## Personal Development

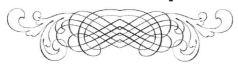

In this section, we present a collection of inspiring quotes that focus on personal development. These wise words will encourage you to invest in yourself, continually learn, and embrace self-improvement. May these quotes inspire you to become the best version of yourself and lead a life filled with growth and self-discovery.

---

"Your level of success will seldom exceed your level of personal development, because success is something you attract by the person you become."
  - Jim Rohn

"A person that has never made a mistake never tried anything new."
  - Albert Einstein

# Growth

"Do good. Give the world the best you have and it may never be enough. Give your best anyway."
- Mother Teresa

"Always Do Your Best. Your best is going to change from moment to moment; it will be different when you are healthy as opposed to sick. Under any circumstance, simply do your best, and you will avoid self-judgment, self-abuse and regret."
- Don Miguel Ruiz

"Mediocrity knows nothing higher than itself, but talent instantly recognized genius."
- Arthur Conan Doyle, The Sign of Fear

"If I really want to improve my situation, I can work on the one thing over which I have control - myself."
- Stephen Covey, The 7 Habits of Highly Effective People

"That which is used strengthens and grows, while that which is not used withers and dies."
- Socrates

"The greatest day in your life and mine is when we take total responsibility for our attitudes. That's the day we truly grow up."
- John Maxwell

"I am only an average man, but, by George, I work harder than any average man."
- Theodore Roosevelt

# Growth

"A person's worth in this world is estimated according to the value he places on himself."
    - Jean De La Bruyere (French Philosopher)

"You are never too old to set another goal on to dream, a new dream."
    - C.S. Lewis

"Personal development is a major time-saver. The better you become, the less time it takes you to achieve your goals."
    - Brian Tracy

"Try not to become a man of success but rather try to become a man of value."
    - Albert Einstein

"You must become the master of your own life, or it will become the master of you."
    - Umbrella Academy S1E4 36:45

"Discipline yourself and others won't need to."
    - John Wooden

"Don't limit your challenges, challenge your limits."
    - Jerry Dunn

"Don't concern yourself with the money. Be of service ... build ... work ... dream ... create! Do this and you'll find there is no limit to the prosperity and abundance that will come to you."
    - Earl Nightengale

# Growth

"I will prepare and someday my chance will come."
- Abraham Lincoln

"Life is growth. If we stop growing, technically and spiritually, we are as good as dead."
- Morihei Ueshiba

"Strength and growth come only through continuous effort and struggle."
- Napoleon Hill

"Be patient with yourself. Self-growth is tender; it's holy ground. There's no greater investment."
- Stephen Covey

"Every day, do something that will inch you closer to a better tomorrow."
- Doug Firebaugh

"The highest reward for a person's toil is not what they get for it, but what they become by it."
- John Ruskin

"Growth is never by mere chance; it is the result of forces working together."
- James Cash Penney

"You cannot dream yourself into a character; you must hammer and forge yourself one."
- James A. Froude

Growth

"Self-growth is a spiral process, doubling back on itself, reassessing and regrouping."
- Julia Cameron

"Invest in yourself, for it will be the best investment you ever make."
- Benjamin Franklin

"Personal growth is not a matter of learning new information but of unlearning old limits."
- Alan Cohen

"Believe in yourself, take on your challenges, dig deep within yourself to conquer fears. Never let anyone bring you down. You got this."
- Chantal Sutherland

## Facing Obstacles & Embracing Change

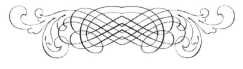

Challenges and changes are an inevitable part of life. This collection of quotes will help you find the strength and courage to face obstacles head-on, embrace change, and turn adversity into opportunity. Let these powerful words guide you through life's twists and turns, and remind you that every struggle can be a catalyst for growth.

"Growth doesn't come from a comfort zone, but from leaving one."
    - Max Brooks, Minecraft: The Island

"Nothing changes until you change, everything changes once you change."
    - Jim Rohn

"To change ourselves effectively, we first had to change our perceptions."
    - Stephen Covey

"You never change your life until you step out of your comfort zone; change begins at the end of your comfort zone."
    - Roy T. Bennett

"When I had nothing to lose, I had everything; when I stopped being who I am, I found myself."
    - Paulo Coelho

"Insanity: doing the same thing over and over again and expecting different results."
    - Albert Einstein

# Growth

"If you change the way you look at things, the things you look at change."
    - Wayne Dyer

"What we fear of doing most is usually what we most need to do."
    - Ralph Waldo Emerson

"Embrace uncertainty. Some of the most beautiful chapters in our lives won't have a title until much later."
    - Bob Goff

"Step by step and the thing is done."
    - Charles Atlas

"Stretching yourself beyond your perceived level of confidence and ability is essential to growth and self-improvement."
    - Brian Tracy

"Be not afraid of growing slowly; be afraid only of standing still."
    - Chinese Proverb

"Most obstacles melt away when we make up our minds to walk boldly through them."
    - Orison Swett Marden

"Challenges make you discover things about yourself that you never really knew."
    - Cicely Tyson

# Growth

"There is no growth without change, no change without fear or loss, and no loss without pain."
  - Rick Warren

"Progress is impossible without change, and those who cannot change their minds cannot change anything."
  - George Bernard Shaw

"Every next level of your life will demand a different you."
  - Leonardo DiCaprio

"Life is change. Growth is optional. Choose wisely."
  - Karen Kaiser Clark

"You will either step forward into growth or you will step back into safety."
  - Abraham Maslow

"The only way that we can live is if we grow. The only way that we can grow is if we change."
  - C. JoyBell C.

"The purpose of life is to live it, to taste experience to the utmost, to reach out eagerly and without fear for newer and richer experience."
  - Eleanor Roosevelt

"The only way to make sense out of change is to plunge into it, move with it, and join the dance."
  - Alan Watts

# Growth

"Change is inevitable. Growth is optional."
- John C. Maxwell

"Life is about growth and exploration, not achieving a fixed state of balance."
- Mel Robbins

"Life is a series of natural and spontaneous changes. Don't resist them; that only creates sorrow. Let reality be reality. Let things flow naturally forward in whatever way they like."
- Lao Tzu

"Challenges are gifts that force us to search for a new center of gravity. Don't fight them. Just find a new way to stand."
- Oprah Winfrey

"Every moment is a fresh beginning."
- T.S. Eliot

"Life is not about waiting for the storm to pass, but learning to dance in the rain."
- Vivian Greene

## Goal Setting and Achievement

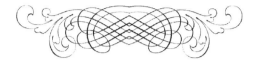

Goals give direction and purpose to our lives. In this section, you'll find a selection of quotes that celebrate the importance of setting and achieving goals. These motivational words will inspire you to dream big, take action, and work relentlessly towards your aspirations. May these quotes fuel your drive to create a fulfilling and successful life.

"Start with the end in mind."
- Stephen Covey

"Destiny is not a matter of chance; it is a matter of choice. It is not something to be waited for; but rather something to be achieved."
- William Jennings Bryan

"If you make the world better in one way, it becomes better in every way."
- William Wilberforce

"It is wonderful how much may be done if we are always doing."
- Thomas Jefferson

# Growth

"Seest thou man diligent in his calling, he shall stand before kings, he shall not stand before mean men."
    - Proverbs 22:29

"According to the commonest principles of human action, no man will do as much for you as you will do for yourself."
    - Marcus Garvey

"It does not matter how slowly you go as long as you do not stop."
    - Confucius

"Progress lies not in enhancing what is, but in advancing toward what will be."
    - Khalil Gibran

"What you do makes a difference, and you have to decide what kind of difference you want to make."
    - Jane Goodall

"Without continual growth and progress, such words as improvement, achievement, and success have no meaning."
    - Benjamin Franklin

"You don't have to be great to start, but you have to start to be great."
    - Zig Ziglar

"The man who moves a mountain begins by carrying away small stones."
    - Confucius

# Growth

"Do something today that your future self will thank you for."
- Sean Patrick Flanery

"Sometimes the smallest step in the right direction ends up being the biggest step of your life."
- unknown

"Your life is an occasion. Rise to it."
- Suzanne Weyn

"Continuous improvement is better than delayed perfection."
- Mark Twain

"Your life only gets better when you get better."
- Brian Tracy

"In times of change, learners inherit the earth, while the learned find themselves beautifully equipped to deal with a world that no longer exists."
- Eric Hoffer

"A dream becomes a goal when action is taken toward its achievement."
- Bo Bennett

"Success is steady progress toward one's personal goals."
- Jim Rohn

"You can't cross the sea merely by standing and staring at the water."
- Rabindranath Tagore

# Growth

"The greater danger for most of us isn't that our aim is too high and we miss it, but that it is too low and we reach it."
    - Michelangelo

"People with goals succeed because they know where they're going."
    - Earl Nightingale

"Set your goals high, and don't stop till you get there."
    - Bo Jackson

"The starting point of all achievement is desire."
    - Napoleon Hill

"The tragedy in life doesn't lie in not reaching your goal. The tragedy lies in having no goal to reach."
    - Benjamin Mays

"The only limit to the height of your achievements is the reach of your dreams and your willingness to work for them."
    - Michelle Obama

"You are never too old to set another goal or to dream a new dream."
    - C.S. Lewis

"The bigger the challenge, the bigger the opportunity for growth."
    - Michael Hyatt

# Growth

"An aim in life is the only fortune worth finding."
    - Robert Louis Stevenson

"The only way to achieve your goals is to bite off more than you can chew, and chew as fast as you can."
    - Paul Hogan

"Set your sights high, the higher the better. Expect the most wonderful things to happen, not in the future but right now. Realize that nothing is too good. Allow absolutely nothing to hamper you or hold you up in any way."
    - Eileen Caddy

"Goals are dreams with deadlines."
    - Diana Scharf

"A goal properly set is halfway reached."
    - Zig Ziglar

"What you get by achieving your goals is not as important as what you become by achieving your goals."
    - Zig Ziglar

"The key to growth is acknowledging your fear of the unknown and jumping in anyway."
    - Jen Sincero

Growth

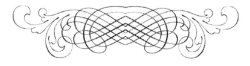

Resilience is the key to overcoming life's challenges and bouncing back from setbacks. These quotes on building resilience will inspire you to cultivate inner strength, adapt to change, and develop a mindset of perseverance. Let these wise words serve as a reminder that you are capable of facing any obstacle and emerging stronger and more resilient.

"Fall down seven times, stand up eight."
- Japanese proverb

"Getting over a painful experience is much like crossing monkey bars. You have to let go at some point before you can move forward."
- C.S. Lewis

"When everything seems to be going against you, remember that the airplane takes off against the wind, not with it."
- Henry Ford

"Being defeated is often a temporary condition. Giving up is what make it permanent."
- Marilyn Vos Savant

# Growth

"Adversity causes some men to break, others to break records."
    - William Arthur Ward

"Someone once gave me a box full of darkness. It took me years to understand this, too was a gift."
    - Mary Oliver

"Never be bullied into silence. Never allow yourself to be made a victim. Accept no one's definition of your life, define yourself."
    - Robert Frost

"Remember nothing that is worthwhile is ever easy."
    - unknown

"There is no sunshine without rain."
    - unknown

"Nobody trips over mountains; it's the small pebbles that cause you to stumble. Pass all the pebbles in your path, and you will find you have crossed the mountain."
    - anonymous

"What comes easy won't always last, and what will last won't come easy."
    - unknown

"You learn more from failure than from success; don't let it stop you; failure builds character."
    - unknown

# Growth

"Once you are really challenged, you find something in yourself. Man doesn't know what he is capable of until he's asked."
- Kofi Annan

"Your big opportunity may be right where you are now."
- Napoleon Hill

"Success is not about where you are but where you're headed, and the direction you're going in is determined by the steps you're taking."
- Zig Ziglar

"You can't have a better tomorrow if you're still thinking about yesterday."
- Charles Kettering

"Without a struggle, there can be no progress."
- Frederick Douglass

"The moment you give up is the moment you let someone else win."
- Kobe Bryant

"Life begins at the end of your comfort zone."
- Neale Donald Walsch

"Growth begins when we begin to accept our own weakness."
- Jean Vanier

# Growth

"The only person you should try to be better than is the person you were yesterday."
- Matty Mullins

"Growth happens when you push yourself out of your comfort zone and embrace the unfamiliar."
- Robin Sharma

"The key to growth is the introduction of higher dimensions of consciousness into our awareness."
- Lao Tzu

"The only real failure in life is the failure to grow from what we go through."
- Mark Manson

"Every day, in every way, I am getting better and better."
- Émile Coué

"Life will only change when you become more committed to your dreams than you are to your comfort zone."
- Billy Cox

"Act the way you'd like to be, and soon you'll be the way you act."
- Leonard Cohen

Growth

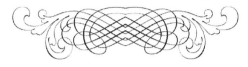
## Positive Thinking

A positive mindset can make a world of difference in your life. In this section, we've compiled quotes that promote positive thinking and an optimistic outlook. These uplifting words will remind you to believe in yourself, focus on the bright side, and harness the power of your thoughts to manifest a brighter future. May these quotes inspire you to cultivate positivity and transform your life for the better.

"The quest for truth is only useful, if you are prepared to take action by what you find."
- Bruce Lee

"Before you give up, remember all the reasons you held on so long."
- unknown

"I would rather have my mind opened by wonder than one closed by belief."
- Gerry Spence

"The real voyage of discovery consists not in seeking new landscapes, but in having new eyes."
- Marcel Proust

# Growth

"It is perception that governs beliefs, attitudes and behaviors."
    - Stephen R. Covey

"On the human chessboard, all moves are possible."
    - Miriam Schiff

"A wise man will make more opportunities than he finds."
    - Francis Bacon

"Don't bother just to be better than your contemporaries or predecessors. Try to be better than yourself."
    - William Faulkner

"True power is grace in response to restrictions and learning to be yourself no matter what situation fate sees to put you in."
    - Cheryl Strauss

"The opportunities of a lifetime must be useful to the lifetime of the opportunity."
    - L. Ravenhill

"Go confidently in the direction of your dreams. Live the life you have imagined."
    - Henry David Thoreau

"Let your dreams be bigger than your fears, and your actions louder than words, and your faith stronger than your feelings."
    - unknown

# Growth

"Success comes in cans, failures in can'ts."
- Wilfred Peterson

"You gotta dance like there's nobody watching, love like you'll never be hurt, sing like there's nobody listening, live like it's heaven on earth."
- William W. Purkey

"Only you can control your future."
- Dr. Seuss

"The best index to a person's character is how they treat people who can't do them any good and how they treat people who can't fight back."
- Abigail Van Buren

"Write it on your heart that every day is the best day in the year."
- Ralph Waldo Emerson

"There's some real utility in gratitude."
- Jordan B. Peterson, 12 Rules for Life

"Personal growth is the process of responding positively to change. It involves risk as you step from the known to the unknown."
- George O. Wood

"There is no growth except in the fulfillment of obligations."
- Antoine de Saint-Exupéry

"Character may be manifested in the great moments, but it is made in the small ones."
- Phillips Brooks

"Life's most persistent and urgent question is, 'What are you doing for others?'"
- Martin Luther King Jr.

"Nearly all men can stand adversity, but if you want to test a man's character, give him power."
- Abraham Lincoln

"If you want to lift yourself up, lift up someone else."
- Booker T. Washington

"Setting an example is not the main means of influencing others; it is the only means."
- Albert Einstein

"Nothing in life has any meaning except the meaning you give it."
- Tony Robbins

"Life is a journey of continuous growth and self-improvement. Embrace the process, and never stop learning."
- unknown

"Your mind is a powerful thing. When you fill it with positive thoughts, your life will start to change."
- unknown

Growth

"Strength shows not only in the ability to persist, but in the ability to start over."
- F. Scott Fitzgerald

"The only way to grow is to challenge yourself."
- Ashley Tisdale

"Small deeds done are better than great deeds planned."
- Peter Marshall

# Focus & Clarity

### Clear Thinking

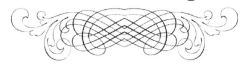

In a world full of distractions and information overload, clear thinking is a powerful tool for personal and professional success. This section brings together quotes that emphasize the importance of mental clarity, simplicity, and the ability to sift through the noise. Let these words inspire you to cultivate a clear mind and make better decisions in every aspect of your life.

---

"How to achieve such anomalies, such alterations and refashioning of reality so what comes out of it are lies, if you like, but lies are more literal than truth."
- unknown

"There is a world of difference between truth and facts, facts can obscure truth."
- Maya Angelou

# Focus & Clarity

"To over analyze is to paralyze."
  - unknown

"Doubt is an uncomfortable condition, but certainty is absurd."
  - Voltaire

"When we believe in lies, we cannot see the truth, so we make thousands of assumptions and we take them as truth. One of the biggest assumptions we make is that the lies we believe are the truth!"
  - Don Miguel Ruiz

"What we wish, we really believe, and what we ourselves think, we imagine other think also"
  - William Shakespeare

"Definition is the companion of clarity; clarity is the guide to your goals."
  - Tony Buzan

"It takes careful observation, and education, and reflection, and communication with others, just to scratch the surface of your beliefs."
  - Jordan B. Peterson, 12 Rules for Life

"Whenever we're afraid, it's because we don't know enough. If we understood enough, we would never be afraid."
  - Earl Nightingale

"Clarity comes from knowing what you want and moving in the direction of it."
- Iyanla Vanzant

"Clarity is the counterbalance of profound thoughts."
- Luc de Clapiers

"Clarity and simplicity are the antidotes to complexity and uncertainty."
- General George S. Patton

"Without clarity, we cannot make informed decisions, solve problems, or communicate effectively."
- Nancy Kline

"Clarity of mind means clarity of passion, too; this is why a great and clear mind loves ardently and sees distinctly what it loves."
- Blaise Pascal

"Confusion is the enemy of progress. Clarity leads to achievement and fulfillment."
- Brian Tracy

"Simplicity is the ultimate sophistication."
- Leonardo da Vinci

"With clarity comes the ability to simplify, and when we simplify, we become more efficient."
- Myles Munroe

# Focus & Clarity

"Clarity is the counterbalance of profound thoughts."
- Luc de Clapiers

"Clarity is power, and knowing where you're going is the first step in getting anywhere."
- Anne Sweeney

"Clarity is the most important thing. If you have a clear vision, even the right people with the right skills can't help you."
- Gail Sheehy

"Be clear about your goal, but be flexible about the process of achieving it."
- Brian Tracy

"Clarity of vision is the key to achieving your objectives."
- Tom Steyer

"A clear vision, backed by definite plans, gives you a tremendous feeling of confidence and personal power."
- Brian Tracy

"Clear thinking requires courage rather than intelligence."
- Thomas Szasz

"Success is not about the destination, it's about the journey."
- Zig Ziglar

"The road to success and the road to failure are almost exactly the same."
- Colin R. Davis

Focus & Clarity

## Decision Making

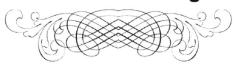

Making decisions is an inevitable part of our daily lives, and the choices we make shape our future. In this section, you'll find quotes that highlight the significance of effective decision-making, encourage you to trust your instincts, and inspire you to take action. Reflect on these words of wisdom to help guide you through life's important crossroads.

"Circumstance does not make the man, it reveals him to himself."
- James Allen

"You'll never find the right things, if you don't let go of the wrong ones."
- unknown

"As I get older I pay less attention to what people say, I just watch what they do."
- Andrew Carnegie

# Focus & Clarity

"If you aim at nothing, you hit nothing"
    - Shang-Chi and the Legend of the Ten Rings

"Without a sense of urgency, desire loses its value."
    - Jim Rohn

"We must be willing to let go of the life we planned so as to have the life that is waiting for us."
    - Joseph Campbell

"It did not really matter what we expect from life, but rather what life expected from us."
    - Viktor Frankl

"The clearer your vision, the more you're able to make better decisions."
    - Brendon Burchard

"Decide what you want, decide what you are willing to exchange for it. Establish your priorities and go to work."
    - H. L. Hunt

"Believe in yourself! Have faith in your abilities! Without a humble but reasonable confidence in your own powers, you cannot be successful or happy."
    - Norman Vincent Peale

"True genius resides in the capacity for the evaluation of uncertain, hazardous, and conflicting information."
    - Winston Churchill

## Focus & Clarity

"Where there is no vision, there is no hope."
  - George Washington Carver

"Do the best you can until you know better. Then when you know better, do better."
  - Maya Angelou

"A lack of clarity could put the brakes on any journey to success."
  - Steve Maraboli

"Stay committed to your decisions, but stay flexible in your approach."
  - Tony Robbins

"Only put off until tomorrow what you are willing to die having left undone."
  - Pablo Picasso

"Successful people do what unsuccessful people are not willing to do. Don't wish it were easier; wish you were better."
  - Jim Rohn

"I attribute my success to this: I never gave or took any excuse."
  - Florence Nightingale

"You cannot make progress without making decisions."
  - Jim Rohn

# Focus & Clarity

"Sometimes it's the smallest decisions that can change your life forever."
    - Keri Russell

"The most difficult thing is the decision to act, the rest is merely tenacity."
    - Amelia Earhart

"When you make a choice, you change the future."
    - Deepak Chopra

"It is our choices that show what we truly are, far more than our abilities."
    - J.K. Rowling

"In order to succeed, we must first believe that we can."
    - Nikos Kazantzakis

"Life is a matter of choices, and every choice you make makes you."
    - John C. Maxwell

"The hardest decisions in life are not between good and bad or right and wrong, but between two goods or two rights."
    - Joe Andrew

"Once you make a decision, the universe conspires to make it happen."
    - Ralph Waldo Emerson

"We make our choices, then our choices make us."
    - Anne Frank

Focus & Clarity

"Trust your instincts, and make judgments on what your heart tells you. The heart will not betray you."
- David Gemmell

"Don't be afraid to make decisions, be afraid of not making them."
- Grant Cardone

"You are one decision away from a totally different life."
- Mark Batterson

"The most important decision you make is to be in a good mood."
- Voltaire

## Focus & Concentration

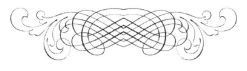

In a world filled with endless distractions, maintaining focus and concentration is essential for achieving our goals. This collection of quotes emphasizes the power of laser-like focus and the importance of honing our concentration skills. Allow these insightful words to inspire you to stay persistent and dedicated in the pursuit of your dreams

# Focus & Clarity

"Things that matter most must never be at the mercy of things that matter least."
    - Johann Wolfgang Von Goethe

"We suffer more often in imagination than in reality."
    - Seneca

"I am the master of my fate, I am the captain of my soul."
    - William Ernest Henley

"The difference between failure and success is doing a thing nearly right and doing a thing exactly right."
    - Edward Simmons

"The key to success is to focus our conscious mind on things we desire not things we fear."
    - Brian Tracy

"The successful warrior is the average man, with laser-like focus."
    - Bruce Lee

"Starve your distractions, feed your focus."
    - unknown

"Clarity is the cradle of power, and focused action is its delivery mechanism."
    - Brendon Burchard

# Focus & Clarity

"Your ability to focus is a skill that can be developed and strengthened over time."
— John Assaraf

"Maintain your focus on what's truly important, and the rest will fall into place."
— Brian Tracy

"Focused, hard work is the real key to success. Keep your eyes on the goal, and just keep taking the next step towards completing it."
— John Carmack

"Where focus goes, energy flows."
— Tony Robbins

"Concentrate all your thoughts upon the work at hand. The sun's rays do not burn until brought to a focus."
— Alexander Graham Bell

"Focusing on one thing and doing it really, really well can get you very far."
— Kevin Systrom

"The key to success is to focus our conscious mind on things we desire, not things we fear."
— Brian Tracy

"Focus on the journey, not the destination. Joy is found not in finishing an activity but in doing it."
— Greg Anderson

# Focus & Clarity

"The successful warrior is the average man, with laser-like focus."
    - Bruce Lee

"Concentration is the secret of strength."
    - Ralph Waldo Emerson

"The power to concentrate was the most important thing. Living without this power would be like opening one's eyes without seeing anything."
    - Haruki Murakami

"Obstacles are those frightful things you see when you take your eyes off your goal."
    - Henry Ford

"One reason so few of us achieve what we truly want is that we never direct our focus; we never concentrate our power."
    - Tony Robbins

"Stay focused, ignore the distractions, and you will accomplish your goals much faster."
    - Joel Osteen

"Clarity and focus are the keys to achieving your dreams and living a life you love."
    - Lewis Howes

"The harder you work for something, the greater you'll feel when you achieve it."
    - unknown

Focus & Clarity

"Your focus determines your reality."
- George Lucas

"Focus on where you want to go, not on what you fear."
- Anthony Robbins

"Success seems to be connected with action. Successful people keep moving. They make mistakes, but they don't quit."
- Conrad Hilton

"Keep your eyes on the stars and your feet on the ground."
- Theodore Roosevelt

"Success is focusing the full power of all you are on what you have a burning desire to achieve."
- Wilfred Peterson

"Work hard in silence, let your success be your noise."
- Frank Ocean

## Purpose and Intention

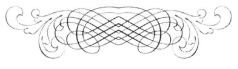

Discovering and embracing our purpose and intention can give our lives meaning and direction. In this section, you'll find thought-provoking quotes that remind you of the

## Focus & Clarity

importance of having a clear vision, being intentional in your actions, and living a life that aligns with your values. Let these quotes guide you on your journey towards living a purposeful and intentional life.

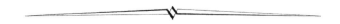

"Success is not the key to happiness. Happiness is the key to success. If you love what you are doing, you will be successful."
- Albert Schweitzer

"A life without cause is a life without effect."
- unknown

"Never stop doing your best just because someone doesn't give you credit."
- unknown

"Unhappiness is not knowing what we want and killing ourselves to get it."
- Don Herold

"Setting goals is the first step in turning the invisible into the visible."
- Tony Robbins

"It doesn't matter where you are coming from. All that matters is where you are going."
- Brian Tracy

"The trouble with not having a goal is that you can spend your life running up and down the field and never score."
    - Bill Copeland

"The most important thing in life is to stop saying 'I wish' and start saying 'I will.' Consider nothing impossible, then treat possibilities as probabilities."
    - Charles Dickens

"The artist is nothing without the gift, but the gift is nothing without work."
    - Émile Zola

"He who has a why to live for can bear almost any how."
    - Friedrich Nietzsche

"You must determine where you are going in your life, because you cannot get there unless you move in that direction. Random wandering will not move you forward. It will instead disappoint and frustrate you and make you anxious and unhappy and hard to get along with (and then resentful, and then vengeful, and then worse)."
    - Jordan B. Peterson, 12 Rules for Life

"Always bear in mind that your own resolution to succeed is more important than any other thing."
    - Abraham Lincoln

"You are now, and you do become, what you think about."
    - Earl Nightengale

# Focus & Clarity

"Follow your passion, be prepared to work hard and sacrifice, and, above all, don't let anyone limit your dreams."
- Donovan Bailey

"The secret of change is to focus all your energy not on fighting the old, but on building the new."
- Socrates

"The more clear and specific your goals, the faster and more efficiently you'll move toward them."
- Zig Ziglar

"Success isn't about how much money you make; it's about the difference you make in people's lives."
- Michelle Obama

"When you have clarity of intention, the universe conspires with you to make it happen."
- Fabienne Fredrickson

"Success means having the courage, the determination, and the will to become the person you believe you were meant to be."
- George A. Sheehan

"The only way to do great work is to love what you do."
- Steve Jobs

"Whatever you can do, or dream you can, begin it. Boldness has genius, power, and magic in it."
- Johann Wolfgang von Goethe

"When you find your path, you must not be afraid. You need to have sufficient courage to make mistakes."
    - Paulo Coelho

"The only way to achieve the impossible is to believe it is possible."
    - Charles Kingsleigh

"Create with the heart; build with the mind."
    - Criss Jami

"Be true to yourself, help others, make each day your masterpiece, make friendship a fine art, drink deeply from good books - especially the Bible, build a shelter against a rainy day, give thanks for your blessings and pray for guidance every day."
    - John Wooden

"Whatever the mind can conceive and believe, the mind can achieve."
    - Napoleon Hill

"Find a purpose to serve, not a lifestyle to live."
    - Criss Jami

"Success is not to be pursued; it is to be attracted by the person you become."
    - Jim Rohn

Focus & Clarity

"Success is liking yourself, liking what you do, and liking how you do it."
 - Maya Angelou

"Success is not counted by how high you have climbed but by how many people you brought with you."
 - Wil Rose

"Success is the ability to go from one failure to another with no loss of enthusiasm."
 - Sir Winston Churchill

"Success is not a destination, but the road that you're on. Being successful means that you're working hard and walking your walk every day."
 - Marlon Wayans

"Success is about creating benefit for all and enjoying the process. If you focus on this and adopt this definition, success is yours."
 - Kelly Kim

"Your time is limited, don't waste it living someone else's life."
 - Steve Jobs

## **Mindfulness & Awareness**

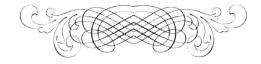

This section features quotes that encourage you to be present, appreciate the moment, and deepen your understanding of yourself and the world around you. Allow these wise words to inspire you to cultivate mindfulness and awareness in your daily life, ultimately leading to greater clarity and focus.

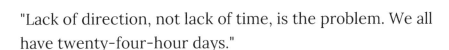

"Lack of direction, not lack of time, is the problem. We all have twenty-four-hour days."
- Zig Ziglar

"Life is easier than you think; all that is necessary is to accept the impossible, do without the indispensable, and bear the intolerable."
- Kathleen Norris

"We can change our circumstances by a mere change of our attitude."
- William James

"I have not special talents. I am passionately curious."
- Albert Einstein

# Focus & Clarity

"If you look for truth, you may find comfort in the end; if you look for comfort you will not get either comfort or truth only soft soap and wishful thinking to begin, and in the end, despair."
    - C.S. Lewis

"Courage is to take a step forward into an area of difficulty without a solution in mind. But yet feeling that victory is ahead."
    - unknown

"Success comes to those who have an entire mountain of gold that they continually mine, not those who find one nugget and try to live on it for fifty years."
    - John C. Maxwell

"I don't really care about this concept happiness, other things are more important."
    - Werner Herzog

"Beliefs are the key to happiness, and to misery."
    - Aaron Beck

"If I quit, I will soon be back where I started, and where I started, I was desperately wishing to be where I am right now."
    - unknown

"The fear of hell is hell itself, and the longing for Heaven is Heaven itself."
    - Kahlil Gibran

## Focus & Clarity

"Man is the universe being conscious with itself."
- unknown

"I like friends who have independent minds because they tend to make you see problems from all angles."
- Nelson Mandela

"People should pursue what they're passionate about. That will make them happier than pretty much anything else."
- Elon Musk

"To persevere is always a reflection of the state of one's inner life, one's philosophy, and one's perspective."
- David Guterson

"Human beings are works in progress that mistakenly think they're finished."
- Dan Gilbert

"Yesterday is history, tomorrow is a mystery, today is a gift of God, which is why we call it the present."
- Bil Keane

"Your life becomes a masterpiece when you learn to master peace."
- Danny Silk

"Self-reflection is the key to clarity. When we have clarity, we can make better choices."
- Deepak Chopra

# Focus & Clarity

"The more of me I be, the clearer I can see."
    - Rachel Archelaus

"True self-discovery begins where your comfort zone ends."
    - Adam Braun

"Only in quiet waters things mirror themselves undistorted. Only in a quiet mind is adequate perception of the world."
    - Hans Margolius

"Focus on the journey, not the destination. Joy is found not in finishing an activity but in doing it."
    - Greg Anderson

"Your ability to generate power is directly proportional to your ability to relax."
    - David Allen

"Do not dwell in the past, do not dream of the future, concentrate the mind on the present moment."
    - Buddha

"The most important thing is to enjoy your life—to be happy—it's all that matters."
    - Audrey Hepburn

"Give light, and the darkness will disappear of itself."
    - Desiderius Erasmus

"Give your dreams all you've got, and you'll be amazed at the energy that comes out of you."
    - William James

# Focus & Clarity

"The difference between a successful person and others is not a lack of strength, not a lack of knowledge, but rather a lack of will."
    - Vince Lombardi

"Your present circumstances don't determine where you can go; they merely determine where you start."
    - Nido Qubein

"Success is a journey, not a destination. The doing is often more important than the outcome."
    - Arthur Ashe

"To succeed in life, you need two things: ignorance and confidence."
    - Mark Twain

"Success is not measured by what you accomplish, but by the opposition you have encountered and the courage with which you have maintained the struggle against overwhelming odds."
    - Orison Swett Marden

"The greatest wealth is to live content with little."
    - Plato

"The ladder of success is best climbed by stepping on the rungs of opportunity."
    - Ayn Rand

Focus & Clarity

## Imagination & Innovation

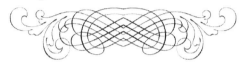

In this subsection, we explore the power of imagination and innovation in sparking creativity. These quotes highlight the importance of embracing our innate ability to dream, envision, and create new ideas, as well as the significance of bringing those ideas to life through innovative actions.

---

"Man's station is only limited to his imagination."
- P.T. Barnum character, The Greatest Showman

"Innovation is creativity with a job to do."
- John Emmerling

"The true sign of intelligence is not knowledge but imagination."
- Albert Einstein

# Creativity

"It's what we storytellers do, we restore order with imagination."
    - Walt Disney's character, Saving Mr. Banks

"What's the thing that's not in the world that should be in the world."
    - Lin-Manuel Miranda

"Creativity is just connecting things. When you ask creative people how they did something, they feel a little guilty because they didn't really do it, they just saw something. It seemed obvious to them after a while. That's because they were able to connect experiences they've had and synthesize new things."
    - Steve Jobs

"Logic will get you from A to B, imagination will take you everywhere."
    - Albert Einstein

"Creativity is the ability to introduce order into the randomness of nature."
    - Eric Hoffer

"Creativity is contagious, pass it on."
    - Albert Einstein

"Imagination is the beginning of creation. You imagine what you desire, you will what you imagine, and at last, you create what you will."
    - George Bernard Shaw

# Creativity

"Creativity is intelligence having fun."
    - Albert Einstein

"I am enough of an artist to draw freely upon my imagination. Imagination is more important than knowledge. Knowledge is limited. Imagination encircles the world."
    - Albert Einstein

"Creative thinking inspires ideas. Ideas inspire change."
    - Barbara Januszkiewicz

"Creativity is the power to connect the seemingly unconnected."
    - William Plomer

"Creativity is the soul's inner compass pointing to the true north of our potential."
    - John C. Maxwell

"Creativity comes from a conflict of ideas."
    - Donatella Versace

"True creativity often starts where language ends."
    - Arthur Koestler

"Imagination is more important than knowledge."
    - Albert Einstein

"Creativity is seeing what everyone else has seen and thinking what no one else has thought."
    - Albert Szent-Györgyi

# Creativity

"Discovering the unexpected is more important than confirming the known."
 - George E. P. Box

"Creativity is the marriage of heart and mind, giving birth to the extraordinary."
 - Rod Judkins

"Creativity requires the courage to let go of certainties."
 - Erich Fromm

"Creativity is the process of having original ideas that have value. It is a process; it's not random."
 - Sir Ken Robinson

"Creativity arises from our ability to see things from many different angles."
 - Keri Smith

"There are only two ways to live your life. One is as though nothing is a miracle. The other is as though everything is a miracle."
 - Albert Einstein

"Creativity is the ability to see relationships where none exist."
 - Thomas Disch

"Believe in your infinite potential. Your only limitations are those you set upon yourself."
 - Roy T. Bennett

# Creativity

"Imagination will often carry us to worlds that never were. But without it, we go nowhere."
    - Carl Sagan

"Without leaps of imagination, or dreaming, we lose the excitement of possibilities. Dreaming, after all, is a form of planning."
    - Gloria Steinem

"Creativity is the ability to bring something new into existence."
    - Peter F. Drucker

"Creativity is the act of turning new and imaginative ideas into reality."
    - Linda Naiman

"Creativity is the process of bringing something new into being."
    - Rollo May

"Imagination is the highest kite one can fly."
    - Lauren Bacall

"Creativity is thinking up new things. Innovation is doing new things."
    - Theodore Levitt

"Creativity is the power to create something from nothing."
    - Henri Matisse

Creativity

"Creativity is the process of discovering new ways to look at the world and solve problems."
- Sir Ken Robinson

"An idea can turn to dust or magic, depending on the talent that rubs against it."
- Bill Bernbach

"Genius is one percent inspiration, ninety-nine percent perspiration."
- Thomas Edison

"Your imagination is your preview of life's coming attractions."
- Albert Einstein

## Artistic Expression

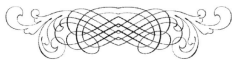

This subsection delves into the world of artistic expression and the profound impact it has on our lives. Through these quotes, we gain insight into the emotions, thoughts, and

# Creativity

experiences that drive artists to create, as well as the transformative power of art on the individual and society.

"When I am finishing a picture, I hold some God-made object up to it - a rock, a flower, the branch of a tree or my hand - as a kind of final test. If the painting stands up beside a thing man cannot make, the painting is authentic. If there is a clash between the two, it is bad art."
  - Marc Chagall 1889-1985 Saturday Evening Post

"Do it again on the next verse, and people think you meant it."
  - Chet Atkins

"Art is an articulator of the soul's uncensored purpose and deepest will."
  - Shaun McNiff, Medicine: Creating a Therapy of the Imagination

"Don't think. Thinking is the enemy of creativity. It's self-conscious, and anything self-conscious is lousy. You can't try to do things. You simply must do things."
  - Ray Bradbury

"Learn the rules like a pro, so you can break them like an artist."
  - Pablo Picasso

"Every act of creation is first an act of destruction."
  - Pablo Picasso

Creativity

"Creativity is a wild mind and a disciplined eye."
    - Dorothy Parker

"The chief enemy of creativity is 'good' sense."
    - Pablo Picasso

"Creativity is allowing yourself to make mistakes. Art is knowing which ones to keep."
    - Scott Adams

"The creative process is a cocktail of instinct, skill, culture, and a highly creative feverishness."
    - Ferran Adrià

"Creative minds are rarely tidy."
    - John W. Gardner

"Painting is poetry that is seen rather than felt, and poetry is painting that is felt rather than seen."
    - Leonardo da Vinci

"Art is not a thing, it is a way."
    - Elbert Hubbard

"Creativity is the way you share your soul with the world."
    - Brene Brown

"The creative adult is the child who survived."
    - Ursula K. Le Guin

"Creativity takes courage."
    - Henri Matisse

# Creativity

"Art washes away from the soul the dust of everyday life."
   - Pablo Picasso

"I dream my painting and I paint my dream."
   - Vincent van Gogh

"The purpose of art is washing the dust of daily life off our souls."
   - Pablo Picasso

"The aim of art is to represent not the outward appearance of things, but their inward significance."
   - Aristotle

"Art must be an expression of love or it is nothing."
   - Marc Chagall

"Art is the daughter of freedom."
   - Friedrich Schiller

"Art should comfort the disturbed and disturb the comfortable."
   - Banksy

"In art, the hand can never execute anything higher than the heart can imagine."
   - Ralph Waldo Emerson

"Where the spirit does not work with the hand, there is no art."
   - Leonardo da Vinci

# Creativity

"Art is not what you see, but what you make others see."
	- Edgar Degas

"Every artist dips his brush in his own soul, and paints his own nature into his pictures."
	- Henry Ward Beecher

"Painting is just another way of keeping a diary."
	- Pablo Picasso

"Art is the only way to run away without leaving home."
	- Twyla Tharp

"Every good painter paints what he is."
	- Jackson Pollock

"To practice any art, no matter how well or badly, is a way to make your soul grow. So do it."
	- Kurt Vonnegut

"The artist vocation is to send light into the human heart."
	- George Sand

"Art is not a handicraft, it is the transmission of feeling the artist has experienced."
	- Leo Tolstoy

"Art and love are the same thing: It's the process of seeing yourself in things that are not you."
	- Chuck Klosterman

"Art is the lie that enables us to realize the truth."
- Pablo Picasso

"A work of art which did not begin in emotion is not art."
- Paul Cezanne

"Great art picks up where nature ends."
- Marc Chagall

"The true work of art is but a shadow of the divine perfection."
- Michelangelo

"Art is to console those who are broken by life."
- Vincent van Gogh

"The essence of all beautiful art, all great art, is gratitude."
- Friedrich Nietzsche

## Embracing Originality

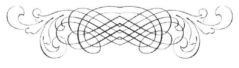

In this subsection, we celebrate the uniqueness of our creative minds. The quotes here emphasize the importance of embracing our originality and allowing our authentic selves to shine through our creations. They remind us that

Creativity

our individuality is an invaluable asset, offering fresh perspectives and possibilities.

"I'm afraid of losing my obscurity. Genuineness only thrives in the dark, like celery."
- Aldus Huxley

"Art is not a mirror held up to reality but a hammer with which to shape it."
- Bertolt Brecht

"Creativity involves breaking out of established patterns in order to look at things in a different way."
- Edward de Bono

"Others have seen what is and asked why. I have seen what could be and asked why not."
- Pablo Picasso, Pablo Picasso: Metamorphoses of the Human Form: Graphic Works, 1895-1972

"If you're not prepared to be wrong, you'll never come up with anything original."
- Ken Robinson

"Originality is born when we break free from the chains of convention and allow our minds to wander into the uncharted territories of our imagination."
- ChatGPT

"To be creative means to be in love with life. You can be creative only if you love life enough that you want to enhance its beauty."
    - Osho

"The creative person is both more primitive and more cultivated, more destructive, a lot madder and a lot saner, than the average person."
    - Frank Barron

"Creativity is not talent but attitude."
    - Jenova Chen

"An idea that is not dangerous is unworthy of being called an idea at all."
    - Oscar Wilde

"Only by going too far can you go far enough."
    - Francis Bacon

"Creativity is the power to reject the past, to change the status quo, and to seek new potential."
    - Ai Weiwei

"The artist is not a special kind of person; rather each person is a special kind of artist."
    - Ananda Coomaraswamy

"Creativity is knowing how to hide your sources"
    - C.E.M. Joad

# Creativity

"If you're always trying to be normal, you will never know how amazing you can be."
- Maya Angelou

"The more you like yourself, the less you are like anyone else, which makes you unique."
- Walt Disney

"Originality is the fine art of remembering what you hear but forgetting where you heard it."
- Laurence J. Peter

"Creativity is an act of defiance."
- Twyla Tharp

"Divergent thinking is the route to creativity."
- Rod Judkins

"The person who follows the crowd will usually go no further than the crowd. The person who walks alone is likely to find himself in places no one has ever seen before."
- Albert Einstein

"Creativity is not a talent; it is a way of operating."
- John Cleese

"The secret to creativity is knowing how to hide your sources."
- anonymous

"In order to be irreplaceable, one must always be different."
- Coco Chanel

# Creativity

"Art is the most intense mode of individualism that the world has known."
    - Oscar Wilde

"The reward for conformity is that everyone likes you but yourself."
    - Rita Mae Brown

"Creativity is the art of hiding your influences."
    - Charles Eames

"The one thing that you have that nobody else has is you. Your voice, your mind, your story, your vision. So write and draw and build and play and dance and live as only you can."
    - Neil Gaiman

"Creativity is the art of making the complicated simple."
    - Edward de Bono

"Originality is the best form of rebellion."
    - Mike Sasso

"You were born an original. Don't die a copy."
    - John Mason

Creativity

## The Creative Process & Mindset

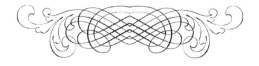

This subsection explores the intricacies of the creative process and the mindset required to tap into our creative potential. The quotes here provide valuable insights into the habits, persistence, and problem-solving skills that are essential for nurturing and sustaining creativity, enabling us to grow and evolve as creators.

"Your mind will answer most questions if you learn to relax and wait for the answer."
 - William S. Burroughs

"To raise new questions, new possibilities, to regard old problems from a new angle, requires creative imagination and makes real advance in science."
 - Albert Einstein

"Problems are hidden opportunities, and constraints can actually boost creativity."
 - Martin Villeneuve

"Making the simple complicated is commonplace; making the complicated simple, awesomely simple, that's creativity."
 - Charles Mingus

# Creativity

"Take the first step in faith. You don't have to see the whole staircase, just take the first step."
- Martin Luther King Jr.

"An essential element of creativity is not being afraid to fail. Failures are the inevitable consequences of experimentation."
- Dr. Edwin Land

"Creativity can solve almost any problem. The creative act, the defeat of habit by originality, overcomes everything."
- George Lois

"Creativity is an act of courage, taking risks and embracing the unknown."
- Georgia O'Keeffe

"Creativity is the key to unlocking the doors of perception."
- Aldous Huxley

"You must do the thing you think you cannot do."
- Eleanor Roosevelt

"Art, in itself, is an attempt to bring order out of chaos."
- Stephen Sondheim

"Vision is the art of seeing what is invisible to others."
- Jonathan Swift

"Creativity is a habit, and the best creativity is the result of good work habits."
- Twyla Tharp

# Creativity

"The opposite of courage in our society is not cowardice... it is conformity."
- Rollo May

"Without freedom, there is no creation."
- Jiddu Krishnamurti

"But everything great is just as difficult to realize as it is rare to find."
- Spinoza

"Every artist was first an amateur."
- Ralph Waldo Emerson

"Creativity is not the finding of a thing, but the making something out of it after it is found."
- James Russell Lowell

"The creative process is a process of surrender, not control."
- Julia Cameron

"Curiosity about life in all its aspects, I think, is still the secret of great creative people."
- Leo Burnett

"Creativity is not a matter of magic, but of hard work and persistent effort."
- Thomas Edison

"Creativity is the ability to create something new, either a new idea, a new thing, or a new way of doing something."
- Mihaly Csikszentmihalyi

"An artist is not paid for his labor but for his vision."
- James Whistler

"Creativity is the alchemy of transforming the ordinary into the extraordinary."
- Rod Judkins

"Creativity is a powerful force that can be harnessed to achieve greatness."
- Elizabeth Gilbert

"An artist cannot fail; it is a success to be one."
- Charles Cooley

## Creative Inspiration

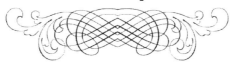

In this final subsection, we delve into the sources of creative inspiration that fuel our imagination and drive our artistic endeavors. These quotes offer glimpses into the myriad ways that creativity can be ignited, reminding us to be open to the wonder, beauty, and curiosity that can spark our most profound and impactful creations.

# Creativity

"creativity is just connecting things."
- Steve Jobs

"Vulnerability is the birthplace of innovation, creativity and change."
- Brene Brown, The Element: How Finding Your Passion Changes Everything

"Mediocrity is always invisible, until passion shows up and exposes it."
- Garlam Cooke

"Fears about yourself dig into your ability to do your best work."
- David Bayles and Ted Orland, Art & Fear: Observations on the Perils (and Rewards) of Artmaking

"Creativity requires input, and that's what research is. You're gathering material with which to build."
- Gene Luen Yang

"Passion is one great force that unleashes creativity, because if you're passionate about something, then you're more willing to take risks."
- Yo-Yo Ma

"An essential aspect of creativity is not being afraid to fail."
- Edwin Land

"You can't use up creativity. The more you use, the more you have."
- Maya Angelou

# Creativity

"Creativity is inventing, experimenting, growing, taking risks, breaking rules, making mistakes, and having fun."
- Mary Lou Cook

"Creativity comes from trust. Trust your instincts. And never hope more than you work."
- Rita Mae Brown

"Creativity is the act of making the invisible visible."
- Paul Klee

"To live a creative life, we must lose our fear of being wrong."
- Joseph Chilton Pearce

"The worst enemy to creativity is self-doubt."
- Sylvia Plath, The Unabridged Journals of Sylvia Plath

"Creativity is the quality that you bring to the activity that you are doing."
- Osho

"In order to be open to creativity, one must have the capacity for constructive use of solitude. One must overcome the fear of being alone."
- Rollo May

"The more you use your creativity, the more it grows and the more valuable it becomes."
- Rod Judkins

"Creativity is piercing the mundane to find the marvelous."
- Bill Moyers

# Creativity

"Your creative spirit is your own personal genie, waiting to grant your every wish."
- Julia Cameron

"Creativity doesn't wait for that perfect moment. It fashions its own perfect moments out of ordinary ones."
- Bruce Garrabrandt

"Your creative work is a manifestation of your energy and consciousness, which are always evolving."
- Rod Judkins

"Creativity is like a lightning bolt; it can strike at any moment."
- Lin-Manuel Miranda

"Ideas are like rabbits. You get a couple and learn how to handle them, and pretty soon you have a dozen."
- John Steinbeck

"Creativity is what happens when you're busy making other plans."
- John Lennon

"The creative process is a voyage of discovery that never ends."
- Orson Welles

"Creativity is a type of learning process where the teacher and the pupil are located in the same individual."
- Arthur Koestler

# Creativity

"Dreams are illustrations from the book your soul is writing about you."
    - Marsha Norman

"Creativity is a natural extension of our enthusiasm."
    - Earl Nightingale

"Inspiration exists, but it has to find you working."
    - Pablo Picasso

"Art is the greatest expression of liberty."
    - Bryant H. McGill

"Creativity is not the possession of some special talent. It's about the willingness to play."
    - John Cleese

"Art is never finished, only abandoned."
    - Leonardo da Vinci

"The job of the artist is always to deepen the mystery."
    - Francis Bacon

"Every child is an artist. The problem is how to remain an artist once we grow up."
    - Pablo Picasso

"The desire to create is one of the deepest yearnings of the human soul."
    - Dieter F. Uchtdorf

# Creativity

"Art enables us to find ourselves and lose ourselves at the same time."
- Thomas Merton

"Creativity is the natural order of life. Life is energy: pure creative energy."
- Julia Cameron

"Your work is to discover your world and then with all your heart give yourself to it."
- Buddha

"Art is a collaboration between God and the artist, and the less the artist does the better."
- André Gide

"Creativity is a spark that ignites the fires of inspiration and fuels the engine of change."
- Scott Belsky

"An artist is a dreamer consenting to dream of the actual world."
- George Santayana

"Creativity is like a muscle. It must be exercised to grow stronger and more agile."
- Julia Cameron

"Life beats down and crushes the soul, and art reminds you that you have one."
- Stella Adler

Creativity

"An artist is always alone – if he is an artist."
- Henry Miller

"Creativity is not a gift; it is a habit, a skill that can be learned, developed and honed."
- Twyla Tharp

## Taking Action & Prioritizing

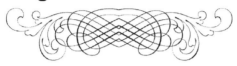

Taking action and prioritizing tasks are key components of productivity. This section focuses on the importance of starting and making progress towards your goals. It emphasizes the need to prioritize tasks based on their importance and impact, ensuring that you direct your energy towards the most essential activities.

---

"The journey of a thousand miles begins with a single step."
  - Chinese proverb

"You are what you do, not what you say you'll do."
  - Carl Jung

"to learn and not to do is really not to learn. To know and not to do is really not to know."
  - Stephen R. Covey, The 7 Habits of Highly Effective People

"You can have a great many ideas in your head, but what makes a difference is the action. Without action upon an idea, there will be no manifestation, no results, and no reward."
- Don Miguel Ruiz, The Four Agreements

"Amateurs sit and wait for inspiration, the rest of us just get up and go to work."
- Stephen King, On Writing: A Memoir of the Craft

"If you spend too much time thinking about a thing, you'll never get it done."
- Bruce Lee

"Action is the foundational key to all success."
- Pablo Picasso

"The way to get started is to quit talking and begin doing."
- Walt Disney

"Do the hard jobs first. The easy jobs will take care of themselves."
- Dale Carnegie

"The key is not to prioritize what's on your schedule, but to schedule your priorities."
- Stephen Covey

"Start by doing what's necessary; then do what's possible, and suddenly you are doing the impossible."
- Francis of Assisi

Productivity

"The key to success is action, and the essential in action is perseverance."
- Sun Yat-sen

"Do not wait; the time will never be 'just right.' Start where you stand, and work with whatever tools you may have at your command, and better tools will be found as you go along."
- George Herbert

"Exploration never stops at failure. Exploration begins with sharing wisdom. Exploration lights the way forward."
- Chinese quotes

"Either you run the day, or the day runs you."
- Jim Rohn

"You cannot change your destination overnight, but you can change your direction overnight."
- Jim Rohn

"The greatest amount of wasted time is the time not getting started."
- Dawson Trotman

"You miss 100% of the shots you don't take."
- Wayne Gretzky

"Action may not always bring happiness, but there is no happiness without action."
- Benjamin Disraeli

# Productivity

"Opportunity is missed by most people because it is dressed in overalls and looks like work."
    - Thomas Edison

"A year from now you may wish you had started today."
    - Karen Lamb

"Don't wait. The time will never be just right."
    - Napoleon Hill

"Begin with the end in mind."
    - Stephen Covey

"Without a sense of urgency, desire loses its value."
    - Jim Rohn

"Stop chasing the money and start chasing the passion."
    - Tony Hsieh

"The secret to getting ahead is getting started."
    - Mark Twain

"Your future is created by what you do today, not tomorrow."
    - Robert Kiyosaki

"Start where you are. Use what you have. Do what you can."
    - Arthur Ashe

"The only place where success comes before work is in the dictionary."
    - Vidal Sassoon

# Productivity

"Setting goals is the first step in turning the invisible into the visible."
    - Tony Robbins

"Do first things first, and second things not at all."
    - Peter Drucker

"Great acts are made up of small deeds."
    - Lao Tzu

"Opportunities don't happen, you create them."
    - Chris Grosser

"Plan your work for today and every day, then work your plan."
    - Margaret Thatcher

"An ounce of action is worth a ton of theory."
    - Friedrich Engels

"The best way to get something done is to begin."
    - unknown

"Action is the real measure of intelligence."
    - Napoleon Hill

"The future depends on what you do today."
    - Mahatma Gandhi

"Things may come to those who wait, but only the things left by those who hustle."
    - Abraham Lincoln

"By failing to prepare, you are preparing to fail."
- Benjamin Franklin

"A goal is a dream with a deadline."
- Napoleon Hill

"Be stubborn about your goals and flexible about your methods."
- unknown

"Don't let yesterday take up too much of today."
- Will Rogers

"Think of many things; do one."
- Portuguese proverb

## Time Management & Efficiency

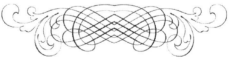

Effective time management and efficiency are crucial for maximizing productivity. This subsection explores strategies for managing time wisely, eliminating distractions, and optimizing productivity. It highlights the significance of planning, organizing, and utilizing time-saving techniques to accomplish more in less time.

# Productivity

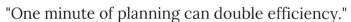

"One minute of planning can double efficiency."
    - Brian Tracy

"What gets measured, gets managed."
    - Peter Drucker, Management Consultant

"Everyone needs deadlines. Even the beavers. They loaf around all summer, but when they are faced with the winter deadline, they work like fury. If we didn't have deadlines, we'd stagnate."
    - Walt Disney

"Work never killed anyone. It's worry that does the damage. And the worry would disappear if we'd just settle down and do the work."
    - Earl Nightingale

"Efficiency is doing things right; effectiveness is doing the right things."
    - Peter Drucker

"Nothing is less productive than to make more efficient what should not be done at all."
    - Peter Drucker

"Time is the scarcest resource and unless it is managed, nothing else can be managed."
    - Peter Drucker

# Productivity

"Lost time is never found again."
- Benjamin Franklin

"Ordinary people think merely of spending time. Great people think of using it."
- Arthur Schopenhauer

"Simplicity boils down to two steps: Identify the essential. Eliminate the rest."
- Leo Babauta

"Time management is not a peripheral activity or skill. It is the core skill upon which everything else in life depends."
- Brian Tracy

"It's not always that we need to do more but rather that we need to focus on less."
- Nathan W. Morris

"Time is a created thing. To say 'I don't have time,' is like saying, 'I don't want to.'"
- Lao Tzu

"Work smarter, not harder."
- Carl Barks

"Never confuse movement with action."
- Ernest Hemingway

"Focus on being productive instead of busy."
- Tim Ferriss

# Productivity

"Time is a resource whose supply is inversely proportional to its demand."
    - Craig D. Lounsbrough

"The trouble is, you think you have time."
    - Buddha

"Work expands to fill the time available for its completion."
    - Cyril Northcote Parkinson

"Don't be fooled by the calendar. There are only as many days in the year as you make use of."
    - Charles Richards

"Time is the most valuable thing a person can spend."
    - Theophrastus

"Those who make the worst use of their time are the first to complain of its brevity."
    - Jean de La Bruyère

"Multitasking is a lie."
    - Gary Keller

"In the realm of time, there is no aristocracy of wealth and no aristocracy of intellect. Genius is never rewarded by even an extra hour a day."
    - Charles W. Eliot

"Procrastination is the thief of time."
    - Edward Young

# Productivity

"Give me six hours to chop down a tree, and I will spend the first four sharpening the axe."
- Abraham Lincoln

"Time is the wisest counselor of all."
- Pericles

"Time flies, but you are the pilot."
- Michael Altshuler

"Until we can manage time, we can manage nothing else."
- Peter Drucker

"Time is the coin of your life. It is the only coin you have, and only you can determine how it will be spent. Be careful lest you let other people spend it for you."
- Carl Sandburg

"The true price of anything you do is the amount of time you exchange for it."
- Henry David Thoreau

"Time = life; therefore, waste your time and waste your life, or master your time and master your life."
- Alan Lakein

"Time is more valuable than money. You can get more money, but you cannot get more time."
- Jim Rohn

"Efficiency is doing better what is already being done."
- Peter Drucker

Productivity

"Do not squander time, for that is the stuff life is made of."
    - Benjamin Franklin

"Know the true value of time; snatch, seize, and enjoy every moment of it."
    - Lord Chesterfield

"Time is what we want most, but what we use worst."
    - William Penn

## Perseverance & Resilience

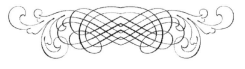

Perseverance and resilience are essential qualities for overcoming challenges and setbacks on the path to productivity. This section emphasizes the importance of staying determined, pushing through obstacles, and bouncing back from failures. It inspires readers to develop a resilient mindset and embrace the power of persistence in achieving their goals.

# Productivity

"Genius is one percent inspiration and 99 percent perspiration."
- Thomas Edison

"The successful among us delay gratification. The successful among us bargain with the future."
- Jordan B. Peterson, 12 Rules for Life

"You've got to get up every morning with determination if you're going to go to bed with satisfaction."
- George Lorimer

"Done is better than perfect."
- Sheryl Sandberg

"Amateurs sit around and wait for inspiration. The rest of us just get up and go to work."
- Chuck Close

"I have not failed. I've just found 10,000 ways that won't work."
- Thomas A. Edison

"Working on the right thing is probably more important than working hard."
- Caterina Fake

"Energy and persistence conquer all things."
- Benjamin Franklin

"Strive for progress, not perfection."
- unknown

Productivity

"Perseverance is the hard work you do after you get tired of doing the hard work you already did."
   - Newt Gingrich

"Don't watch the clock; do what it does. Keep going."
   - Sam Levenson

"Real progress happens when we push ourselves to take the next step, even when we don't feel like it."
   - Shane Parrish

"The only way around is through."
   - Robert Frost

"Success is the child of audacity."
   - Benjamin Disraeli

"Efforts and courage are not enough without purpose and direction."
   - John F. Kennedy

"Success is the result of perfection, hard work, learning from failure, loyalty, and persistence."
   - Colin Powell

"It does not matter how slowly you go as long as you do not stop."
   - Confucius

"Keep going. Everything you need will come to you at the perfect time."
   - unknown

# Productivity

"Continuous effort — not strength or intelligence — is the key to unlocking our potential."
- Winston Churchill

"Many of life's failures are people who did not realize how close they were to success when they gave up."
- Thomas Edison

"It's not whether you get knocked down, it's whether you get back up."
- Vince Lombardi

"A river cuts through a rock, not because of its power, but because of its persistence."
- Jim Watkins

"Champions keep playing until they get it right."
- Billie Jean King

"To succeed, you have to do something and be very bad at it for a while. You have to look bad before you can look really good."
- Barbara DeAngelis

"Tough times never last, but tough people do."
- Robert H. Schuller

"Ever tried. Ever failed. No matter. Try again. Fail again. Fail better."
- Samuel Beckett

Productivity

"The best way out is always through."
- Robert Frost

"You just can't beat the person who never gives up."
- Babe Ruth

"We may encounter many defeats, but we must not be defeated."
- Maya Angelou

"Perseverance is failing 19 times and succeeding the 20th."
- Julie Andrews

"When everything seems to be going against you, remember that the airplane takes off against the wind, not with it."
- Henry Ford

## Mindset and Focus

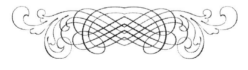

A productive mindset and laser-like focus are vital for accomplishing tasks efficiently. This subsection explores the power of mindset in enhancing productivity, including cultivating a positive attitude, maintaining focus, and adopting a growth mindset. It encourages readers to

Productivity

harness their mental strength and develop a focused mindset to achieve their desired outcomes.

"Act but do not be attached to the fruits of your actions."
    - Buddha

"What you are called to do you will love the most."
    - Rick Joyner

"Inspiration is the windfall from hard work and focus."
    - Helen Hanson

"I am ready to go. Ready to do my job to the best of my abilities. I am focused only on the essential (to the exclusion of all else). I will make only pragmatic decisions. I will not allow myself to be distracted. I will not allow my mind to linger on that which is unimportant. I will not rely on anyone or anything. I will not be vulnerable to mistakes….. [edit at the end of the movie] I will share their burdens as they will share mine."
    - Ad Astra 2019 intro

"Exceptional things come when passion comes first."
    - unknown

"The day is always he who works with serenity and great aim."
    - Ralph Waldo Emerson

Productivity

"There are always two businesses you've got to manage: The business you're in, and the business you're becoming. Always do something to innovate, change or improve."
    - Tony Robbins

"I don't know why we are here, but I'm pretty sure that it is not in order to enjoy ourselves."
    - Ludwig Wittgenstein

"Talkers are usually more articulate than doers, since talk is their specialty."
    - Thomas Sowell

"Talent without genius comes to little. Genius without talent comes to nothing."
    - Paul Valery

"Absorb what is useful, discard what is not, add what is uniquely your own."
    - Bruce Lee

"Productivity is less about what you do with your time and more about how you run your mind."
    - Robin Sharma

"Realize that now, in this moment of time, you are creating. You are creating your next moment. That is what's real."
    - Sara Paddison

"Today's productivity determines tomorrow's success."
    - Myles Munroe

"Your work is going to fill a large part of your life, and the only way to be truly satisfied is to do what you believe is great work. And the only way to do great work is to love what you do."
    - Steve Jobs

"The purpose of life is not to be happy—but to matter, to be productive, to be useful, to have it make some difference that you lived at all."
    - Leo Rosten

"Once you have mastered time, you will understand how true it is that most people overestimate what they can accomplish in a year – and underestimate what they can achieve in a decade!"
    - Tony Robbins

"Optimism is a happiness magnet. If you stay positive, good things and good people will be drawn to you."
    - Mary Lou Retton

"Productivity is not just about doing more. It is about creating more impact with less work."
    - Prerna Malik

"Productivity is the ability to do more in the same amount of time. We all have the same 24 hours in a day, but some people can achieve much more during these hours than others."
    - Kevin Kruse

Productivity

"Focus on what matters and let go of what doesn't."
- unknown

"Productivity is not just about working harder, it's about working on the right things."
- Michael Hyatt

"Success is a state of mind. If you want success, start thinking of yourself as a success."
- Joyce Brothers

"Success is the progressive realization of a worthy goal or ideal."
- Earl Nightingale

"Focus on the things that matter and let go of the things that don't."
- Bruce Lee

"Investing in yourself is the best investment you can make."
- Warren Buffett

"Concentrate all your thoughts upon the work in hand. The sun's rays do not burn until brought to a focus."
- Alexander Graham Bell

"Productivity is the deliberate, strategic investment of your time, talent, intelligence, energy, resources, and opportunities in a manner calculated to move you measurably closer to meaningful goals."
- Dan S. Kennedy

"The only thing standing between you and your goal is the story you keep telling yourself as to why you can't achieve it."
    - Jordan Belfort

## **Balance and Simplicity**

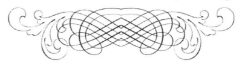

Balancing productivity with well-being and simplicity is crucial for sustainable success. This section highlights the significance of creating a healthy work-life balance, setting boundaries, and simplifying routines. It promotes the idea that productivity is not just about being busy but also about finding harmony, reducing stress, and embracing simplicity in order to lead a fulfilling and productive life.

"Make no mistake about it. Bad habits are called 'bad' for a reason. They kill our productivity and creativity. They slow us down. They hold us back from achieving our goals. And they're detrimental to our health."
    - John Rampton

# Productivity

"Even so every good tree bringeth forth good fruit; but a corrupt tree bringeth forth evil fruit. ... Every tree that does not bear good fruit is cut down and thrown into the fire."
- Matthew 7:17-19

"How might my life be better with less?"
- The Minimalist (documentary)

"Productivity is never an accident. It is always the result of a commitment to excellence, intelligent planning, and focused effort."
- Paul J. Meyer

"Force means shifts in accumulated energy or momentum. Skillful warriors are able to allow the force of momentum to seize victory for them without exerting their strength"
- Art of War

"Don't mistake activity with achievement."
- John Wooden

"Productivity growth, however it occurs, has a disruptive side to it. In the short term, most things that contribute to productivity growth are very painful."
- Janet Yellen

"Don't count the days, make the days count."
- Muhammad Ali

"Make each day your masterpiece."
- John Wooden

# Productivity

"Stop measuring days by degree of productivity and start experiencing them by degree of presence."
- Alan Watts

"The least productive people are usually the ones who are most in favor of holding meetings."
- Thomas Sowell

"Life is too complicated not to be orderly."
- Martha Stewart

"The way we measure productivity is flawed. People checking their BlackBerry over dinner is not the measure of productivity."
- Timothy Ferriss

"Clutter is nothing more than postponed decisions."
- Barbara Hemphill

"Time you enjoy wasting is not wasted time."
- Marthe Troly-Curtin

"Your ability to discipline yourself to use your time well and to keep your life on schedule is the primary measure of your potential for success."
- Brian Tracy

"Productivity is being able to do things that you were never able to do before."
- Franz Kafka

Productivity

"Time is at once the most valuable and the most perishable of all our possessions."
    - John Randolph

"It's not the hours you put in your work that counts, it's the work you put in the hours."
    - Sam Ewing

"Productivity is a measure of how much you accomplish, not how busy you are."
    - Robin Sharma

"Be like a postage stamp. Stick to one thing until you get there."
    - Josh Billings

"Productivity is not about doing more. It's about effectiveness."
    - Chris Bailey

"Success is a lousy teacher. It seduces smart people into thinking they can't lose."
    - Bill Gates

"You can't build a reputation on what you are going to do."
    - Henry Ford

"Success usually comes to those who are too busy to be looking for it."
    - Henry David Thoreau

Productivity

"Stressing output is the key to improving productivity while looking to increase activity can result in just the opposite."
- Paul Gauguin

"Manage your energy, not your time."
- Tony Schwartz

## Integrity & Honesty

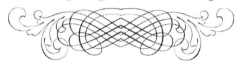

This subsection explores the core values of integrity and honesty, emphasizing the importance of truthfulness, sincerity, and adherence to strong moral principles. These quotes will inspire you to remain steadfast in your beliefs and always choose the path of honesty, even in the face of adversity.

---

"It's not a lie that passes through the mind, but the lie that sinks in and settles in it, that does damage."
  - Francis Bacon, essays

"Nothing ruins the truth like stretching it."
  - attributed to Walter Scott

"Conceal a flaw, and the world will imagine the worst."
  - Marcus Aurelius

## Virtue & Character

"Weakness of attitude becomes weakness of character."
- Albert Einstein

"Be so true to thyself, as thou be not false to others."
- Francis Bacon

"And, after all, what is a lie? 'Tis but the truth in masquerade."
- Lord Byron, Don Juan

"When truth and right are hand in hand, a statement will bear repetition."
- Confucius

"Integrity is doing the right thing when no one is watching."
- unknown

"We should never resent truth even when it hurts."
- Frank Herbert

"When truth and right are hand in hand, a statement will bear repetition."
- Confucius

"Be so true to thyself, as thou be not false to others."
- Francis Bacon

"We should never resent truth even when it hurts."
- Frank Herbert

"By mercy and truth iniquity is purged."
- Proverbs 16:6

## Virtue & Character

"Integrity is doing the right thing, even when no one is watching."
- C.S. Lewis

"A person reveals his character by nothing so clearly as the joke he resents."
- Georg Christoph Lichtenberg

"The best revenge is to be unlike him who performed the injury."
- Marcus Aurelius

"You should not honor men more than truth."
- Plato

"The test of a man's character is what he would do if he knew he would never be found out."
- Thomas B. Macaulay

"Our character is but the stamp on our souls of the free choices of good and evil we have made through life."
- John C. Geikie

"Your character is the sum of all your thoughts, actions, and habits."
- Napoleon Hill

"A man's reputation is the opinion people have of him; his character is what he really is."
- Jack Miner

# Virtue & Character

"Virtue is not left to stand alone. He who practices it will have neighbors."
    - Confucius

"Virtue is its own reward." - Cicero "Character is a diamond that scratches every other stone."
    - Cyrus A. Bartol

"Character is the indelible mark that determines the only true value of all people and all their work."
    - Orison Swett Marden

"The true test of a man's character is what he does when no one is watching."
    - John Wooden

"Character is much easier kept than recovered."
    - Thomas Paine

"Reputation is what men and women think of us; character is what God and angels know of us."
    - Thomas Paine

Virtue & Character

## Kindness & Compassion

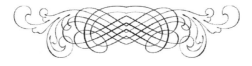

Within this subsection, you will find quotes that showcase the power of kindness and compassion. These timeless words of wisdom remind us of the significance of empathy, understanding, and the ability to care for others, allowing us to build stronger connections and contribute to a better world.

"Being deeply loved by someone gives you strength, while loving someone deeply gives you courage."
    - Lao Tzu

"You cannot do a kindness too soon, for you never know how soon it will be too late."
    - Ralph Waldo Emerson

"Show respect even to people who don't deserve it not as a reflection of their character, but as a reflection of yours."
    - unknown

"Careless means to care less, careful means to be full of caring."
    - unknown

## Virtue & Character

"Love is not what we say it's what we do."
 - unknown

"Love is a fruit in season at all times, and within reach of every hand."
 - Mother Teresa

"Duty makes us do things well, but love makes us do them beautifully."
 - Phillips Brooks

"The smallest act of kindness is worth more than the grandest intention."
 - Oscar Wilde

"Kindness in words creates confidence. Kindness in thinking creates profoundness. Kindness in giving creates love."
 - Lao Tzu

"The only reward of virtue is virtue; the only way to have a friend is to be one."
 - Ralph Waldo Emerson

"Only a life lived for others is a life worthwhile."
 - Albert Einstein

"Kindness is a language which the deaf can hear and the blind can see."
 - Mark Twain

"Virtue is its own reward."
 - Cicero

Virtue & Character

"No act of kindness, no matter how small, is ever wasted."
    - Aesop

"Forgiveness is the attribute of the strong."
    - Mahatma Gandhi

"Tenderness and kindness are not signs of weakness and despair, but manifestations of strength and resolution."
    - Kahlil Gibran

"Compassion is the radicalism of our time."
    - Dalai Lama

"If you want others to be happy, practice compassion. If you want to be happy, practice compassion."
    - Dalai Lama

"Be kind, for everyone you meet is fighting a hard battle."
    - Plato

"Character is built by striving to be kind, not famous."
    - Andy Rooney

"We can't help everyone, but everyone can help someone."
    - Ronald Reagan

"A warm smile is the universal language of kindness."
    - William Arthur Ward

"Wherever there is a human in need, there is an opportunity for kindness and to make a difference."
    - Kevin Heath

Virtue & Character

"Character is power."
— Booker T. Washington

"Kindness can become its own motive. We are made kind by being kind."
— Eric Hoffer

"You cannot do a kindness too soon, for you never know how soon it will be too late."
— Ralph Waldo Emerson

"To be kind is more important than to be right. Many times, what people need is not a brilliant mind that speaks but a special heart that listens."
— F. Scott Fitzgerald

## Courage & Bravery

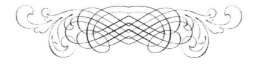

This collection of quotes highlights the importance of courage and bravery in overcoming obstacles, facing fears, and pursuing our dreams. These powerful words encourage us to be resilient and steadfast, inspiring us to embrace our inner strength and persevere through life's challenges.

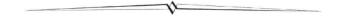

Virtue & Character

"Faith is taking the first step even when you don't see the whole staircase."
- Dr. Martin Luther King

"True love doesn't mean being inseparable. It means being separated and nothing changes."
- unknown

"Love is a fruit in season at all times, and within reach of every hand."
- Mother Teresa

"It is not the critic who counts... The credit belongs to the man who is actually in the arena."
- Theodore Roosevelt

"Success is not final, failure is not fatal: It is the courage to continue that counts."
- Winston Churchill

"Virtue is bold, and goodness never fearful."
- William Shakespeare

"Courage is resistance to fear, mastery of fear, not absence of fear."
- Mark Twain

"Courage is what it takes to stand up and speak; courage is also what it takes to sit down and listen."
- Winston Churchill

## Virtue & Character

"A hero is no braver than an ordinary man, but he is brave five minutes longer."
- Ralph Waldo Emerson

"He who is brave is free."
- Seneca

"It is better to be a lion for a day than a sheep all your life."
- Elizabeth Kenny

"Courage is contagious. When a brave man takes a stand, the spines of others are often stiffened."
- Billy Graham

"To dare is to lose one's footing momentarily. Not to dare is to lose oneself."
- Søren Kierkegaard

"Bravery is the capacity to perform properly even when scared half to death."
- Omar N. Bradley

"Without courage, wisdom bears no fruit."
- Baltasar Gracian

"It takes a great deal of bravery to stand up to our enemies, but just as much to stand up to our friends."
- J.K. Rowling

"Courage is grace under pressure."
- Ernest Hemingway

Virtue & Character

"Courage is not simply one of the virtues, but the form of every virtue at the testing point."
  - C.S. Lewis

"He who is brave is free."
  - Lucius Annaeus Seneca

"Fortune favors the brave."
  - Terence

## Humility & Modesty

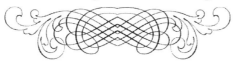

This subsection focuses on humility and modesty, two virtues that encourage us to remain grounded, recognize our limitations, and appreciate the contributions of others. These quotes serve as a reminder to practice consideration for others, embrace our imperfections, and cultivate an attitude of gratitude.

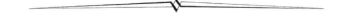

"Confidence is silent, insecurities are loud."
  - unknown

## Virtue & Character

The Master said, " When you see a worth [person], think of becoming equal to him; when you see an unworthy person, survey yourself within."
- Confucius

"Seek wisdom of the ages but look on the world through the eyes of a child."
- Ron Wild

"Confidence is ignorance. If you're feeling cocky, it's because there's something you don't know."
- Eoin Colfer, Artemis Fowl

"Modesty is the color of virtue."
- Diogenes

"Great minds discuss ideas; average minds discuss events; small minds discuss people."
- Eleanor Roosevelt

"Never bend your head. Always hold it high. Look the world straight in the eye."
- Helen Keller

"Pride makes us artificial and humility makes us real."
- Thomas Merton

"The greatest ornament of an illustrious life is modesty and humility, which go a great way in the character even of the most exalted princes."
- Plutarch

# Virtue & Character

"Character is higher than intellect. A great soul will be strong to live as well as think."
    - Ralph Waldo Emerson

"Humility is not thinking less of yourself, it's thinking of yourself less."
    - C.S. Lewis

"Do you wish to rise? Begin by descending. You plan a tower that will pierce the clouds? Lay first the foundation of humility."
    - Saint Augustine

"There is no respect for others without humility in one's self."
    - Henri Frederic Amiel

"Modesty is the gentle art of enhancing your charm by pretending not to be aware of it."
    - Oliver Herford

"Humility and knowledge in poor clothes excel pride and ignorance in costly attire."
    - William Penn

"The proud man can learn humility, but he will be proud of it."
    - Mignon McLaughlin

"None are so empty as those who are full of themselves."
    - Benjamin Whichcote

Virtue & Character

"Modesty is a learned adaptation. It's stuck on like decals. As soon as we cut our hair, as soon as we buy an Aztec sweater and promise we'll never compromise, we begin to die a slow bourgeois spiritual death."
- David Mamet

"A great man is always willing to be little."
- Ralph Waldo Emerson

"True knowledge exists in knowing that you know nothing."
- Socrates

"Humility is the solid foundation of all virtues."
- Confucius

## Responsibility & Accountability

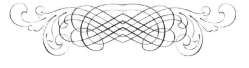

In this subsection, you will find quotes that emphasize the importance of taking responsibility for our actions and being accountable for our choices. These thought-provoking words inspire us to own our mistakes, learn from them, and grow as individuals while contributing positively to society.

# Virtue & Character

"Waste no more time arguing about what a good man should be. Be one."
 - Marcus Aurelius

"We kill people who kill people to show that killing people is wrong."
 - anonymous

"When you have erred, be not afraid of correcting yourself."
 - Confucius

"To enjoy the things we ought and to hate the things we ought has the greatest bearing on excellence of character."
 - Aristotle

"Without virtue, it is difficult to bear gracefully the honors of high office."
 - Chinese Proverb

"To educate a person in the mind but not in morals is to educate a menace to society."
 - Theodore Roosevelt

"A good character is more valuable than material possessions, fame, or achievements."
 - Benjamin Franklin

## Virtue & Character

"Character is the sum and total of a person's choices."
- P.B. Fitzwater

"Character is a quality that embodies many important traits, such as integrity, courage, perseverance, confidence, and wisdom. Unlike your fingerprints that you are born with and can't change, character is something that you create within yourself and must take responsibility for changing."
- Jim Rohn

"Character is the firm foundation stone upon which one must build to win respect. Just as no worthy building can be erected on a weak foundation, so no lasting reputation worthy of respect can be built on a weak character."
- R. C. Samsel

"Character is like a window and those who look in, will see the truth."
- unknown

"Your character is the result of thousands of choices you make each day, and those choices will ultimately determine your destiny."
- unknown

"In the long run, we shape our lives, and we shape ourselves. The process never ends until we die. And the choices we make are ultimately our own responsibility."
- Eleanor Roosevelt

# Virtue & Character

"Character is what emerges from all the little things you were too busy to do yesterday, but did anyway."
- Mignon McLaughlin

"You cannot escape the responsibility of tomorrow by evading it today."
- Abraham Lincoln

"Accountability is the glue that ties commitment to the result."
- Bob Proctor

"Accept responsibility for your life. Know that it is you who will get you where you want to go, no one else."
- Les Brown

"A sign of wisdom and maturity is when you come to terms with the realization that your decisions cause your rewards and consequences. You are responsible for your life, and your ultimate success depends on the choices you make."
- Denis Waitley

"The moment you take responsibility for everything in your life is the moment you can change anything in your life."
- Hal Elrod

"The greatest day in your life and mine is when we take total responsibility for our attitudes. That's the day we truly grow up."
- John C. Maxwell

## Virtue & Character

"Hold yourself responsible for a higher standard than anybody else expects of you. Never excuse yourself."
- Henry Ward Beecher

"If you take responsibility for yourself, you will develop a hunger to accomplish your dreams."
- Les Brown

"The price of greatness is responsibility."
- Winston Churchill

"When you blame others, you give up your power to change."
- Robert Anthony

"We are made wise not by the recollection of our past, but by the responsibility for our future."
- George Bernard Shaw

"Responsibility equals accountability equals ownership. And a sense of ownership is the most powerful weapon a team or organization can have."
- Pat Summitt

"Responsibility is the price of freedom."
- Elbert Hubbard

"You are always responsible for how you act, no matter how you feel. Remember that."
- Robert Tew

Virtue & Character

## **Patience & Persistence**

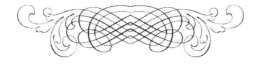

This collection of quotes underscores the value of patience and persistence in overcoming obstacles and achieving our goals. These wise words remind us of the power of perseverance, the importance of staying focused, and the rewards that come from unwavering determination.

"Persistence is the twin sister of excellence. One is a matter of quality; the other, is a matter of time."
  - Marabel Morgan

"Virtue is not a mushroom, that springeth up of itself in one night when we are asleep, or regard it not; but a delicate plant, that groweth slowly and tenderly, needing much pains to cultivate it, much care to guard it, much time to mature it, in our untoward soil, in this world's unkindly weather."
  - Isaac Barrow

"Good character is not formed in a week or a month. It is created little by little, day by day. Protracted and patient effort is needed to develop good character."
  - Heraclitus

# Virtue & Character

"We have two ears and one mouth so that we can listen twice as much as we speak."
    - Epictetus

"Character is the ability to carry out a good resolution long after the excitement of the moment has passed."
    - Cavett Robert

"Character consists of what you do on the third and fourth tries."
    - James A. Michener

"Strength is like a river that cuts through a rock, not because of its power, but its persistence."
    - unknown

"Patience, persistence, and perspiration make an unbeatable combination for success."
    - Napoleon Hill

"Persistence can change failure into extraordinary achievement."
    - Matt Biondi

"With time and patience, the mulberry leaf becomes a silk gown."
    - Chinese Proverb

"Patience is not the ability to wait, but the ability to keep a good attitude while waiting."
    - Joyce Meyer

Virtue & Character

"Never give up on something that you can't go a day without thinking about."
- Winston Churchill

"The two most powerful warriors are patience and time."
- Leo Tolstoy

"Endurance is not just the ability to bear a difficult thing, but to turn it into glory."
- William Barclay

"Perseverance is not a long race; it is many short races one after the other."
- Walter Elliot

"The key to everything is patience. You get the chicken by hatching the egg, not by smashing it."
- Arnold H. Glasow

"The greatest oak was once a little nut who held its ground."
- anonymous

"Patience is passion tamed."
- Lyman Abbot

"The secret of patience is doing something else in the meantime."
- Croft M. Pentz

"Rivers know this: there is no hurry. We shall get there someday."
- A.A. Milne

"Patience is a virtue heavy in wait."
- unknown

## Wisdom and Discipline

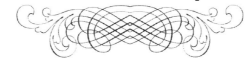

Delve into the essence of wisdom and the power of discipline. This section provides insights that can serve as compass points in life. Wisdom can help you navigate challenges gracefully, make sound decisions, and live a life of purpose. Discipline will help keep you on this pathway to success.

"Principles are what you fight for, most men go through a lifetime unchallenged ... they have so few unfriendly arenas in which to test themselves."
- Frank Herbert

"It is the nature of the wise to resist pleasures, but the foolish to be a slave to them."
- Epictetus

# Virtue & Character

"Wealth is the slave of a wise man and the master of a fool."
    - Seneca

"Science is organized knowledge. Wisdom is organized life."
    - Immanuel Kant

"A wise man will make more opportunities than he finds."
    - Francis Bacon, of ceremonies and respects

"There is no fear in love, but perfect love drives out fear."
    - unknown

"Wise men store up knowledge, but the mouth of the fool is imminent ruin."
    - Proverbs 10:14

"Principles are what you fight for, most men go through a lifetime unchallenged ... they have so few unfriendly arenas in which to test themselves."
    - Frank Herbert

"Wealth is a tool for freedom, but the pursuit of wealth is a way to slavery."
    - Frank Herbert

"A fountain of life is the mouth of the just, but the mouth of the wicked conceals violence."
    - Proverbs 10:11

"Intellectual passion drives out sensuality."
    - Leonardo da Vinci

## Virtue & Character

"Virtue consists, not in abstaining from vice, but in not desiring it."
- George Bernard Shaw

"Adversity is the first path to truth."
- Lord Byron

"A short mouth gathers no foot."
- unknown

"Choose a job you love, and you will never have to work a day in your life."
- Confucius

"Your character is your destiny."
- Heraclitus

"Wise men store up knowledge, but the mouth of the fool is imminent ruin."
- Proverbs 10:14

"A man is but the product of his thoughts; what he thinks, he becomes."
- Mahatma Gandhi

"By associating with wise people, you will become wise yourself."
- Menander

"Character is the result of a system of stereotyped principles."
- Heraclitus

# Virtue & Character

"Happiness is the highest form of wisdom."
- Jacqueline Schiff

"Your character will be what you yourself choose to make it."
- John Lubbock

"Character is that which reveals moral purpose, exposing the class of things a man chooses or avoids."
- Aristotle

"Virtue is the golden mean between two vices, the one of excess and the other of deficiency."
- Aristotle

"Virtue is to the soul what health is to the body."
- François de La Rochefoucauld

"Character is the result of two things: mental attitude and the way we spend our time."
- Elbert Hubbard

"The function of wisdom is to discriminate between good and evil."
- Cicero

"Character may almost be called the most effective means of persuasion."
- Aristotle

"A short mouth gathers no foot."
- unknown

## Virtue & Character

"Self-discipline is the key to personal greatness. It is the magic quality that opens all doors for you and makes everything else possible."
 - Brian Tracy

"The doorstep to the temple of wisdom is a knowledge of our own ignorance."
 - Benjamin Franklin

"Virtue is the harmony of the soul."
 - Pythagoras

"The only true wisdom is in knowing you know nothing."
 - Socrates

"Discipline is the bridge between goals and accomplishment."
 - Jim Rohn

"The truest wisdom is a resolute determination."
 - Napoleon Bonaparte

"Wisdom is the reward you get for a lifetime of listening when you'd have preferred to talk."
 - Doug Larson

"The first and greatest victory is to conquer yourself."
 - Plato

"The greatest wisdom is seeing through appearances."
 - Atisha

Virtue & Character

"Wisdom is the right use of knowledge. To know is not to be wise. Many men know a great deal and are all the greater fools for it."
- Charles Spurgeon

## Freedom & Hope

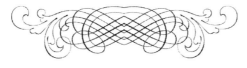

Within this subsection, you will find quotes that celebrate the power of freedom and hope, reminding us of the importance of nurturing our dreams, fighting for our beliefs, and remaining optimistic in the face of adversity. These inspirational words will help us stay resilient and focused on creating a brighter future.

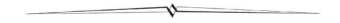

"Freedom is the recognition that no single person, no single authority or government has a monopoly on the truth. It is the right to put forth an idea scoffed at by the experts and watch it catch fire among the people."
- Ronald Regan in Moscow State University 1988

# Virtue & Character

"Hope is not the conviction that something will turn out well, but the certainty that something makes sense, regardless of how it turns out."
- Vaclav Havel

"Hope is not the conviction that something will turn out well, but the certainty that something makes sense, regardless of how it turns out."
- Vaclav Havel

"Your opponents would love you to believe that it's hopeless, that you have no power, that there's no reason to act, that you can't win. Hope is a gift you don't have to surrender, a power you don't have to throw away."
- Rebecca Solnit

"In the end, we will remember not the words of our enemies, but the silence of our friends."
- Martin Luther King Jr.

"I hope that you will be treated unfairly, so that you will come to know the value of justice."
- John Roberts

"The secret of encouragement is hope."
- John Maxwell

"Hope is a good thing, maybe the best of things, and no good thing ever dies."
- Stephen King

Virtue & Character

"Hope is a waking dream."
    - Aristotle

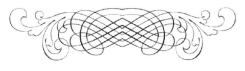

This final subsection is a collection of quotes that emphasize the importance of cultivating strong character and embracing virtue in our daily lives. These powerful words inspire us to make conscious choices, develop good habits, and strive for personal excellence, shaping our destiny and leaving a lasting impact on the world around us.

"Virtue is more to be feared than vice because its excesses are not subject to the regulation of conscience."
    - Adam Smith

"Virtue is the fountain whence honor springs."
    - Christopher Marlowe

"Character is what you are in the dark."
    - Dwight L. Moody

## Virtue & Character

"The only way to deal with an unfree world is to become so absolutely free that your very existence is an act of rebellion."
— Albert Camus

"The only thing necessary for the triumph of evil is for good men to do nothing."
— Edmund Burke

"Character, in the long run, is the decisive factor in the life of an individual and of nations alike."
— Theodore Roosevelt

"For to be free is not merely to cast off one's chains, but to live in a way that respects and enhances the freedom of others."
— Nelson Mandela

"We must accept finite disappointment, but never lose infinite hope."
— Martin Luther King Jr.

"Freedom is not worth having if it does not include the freedom to make mistakes."
— Mahatma Gandhi

"Virtue is more clearly shown in the performance of fine actions than in the non-performance of base ones."
— Aristotle

Virtue & Character

"Freedom is nothing else but a chance to be better."
- Albert Camus

"The only real prison is fear, and the only real freedom is freedom from fear."
- Aung San Suu Kyi

"Virtue is not left to stand alone. He who practices it will have neighbors."
- Confucius

"Freedom lies in being bold."
- Robert Frost

"Virtue is more to be feared than vice because its excesses are not subject to the regulation of conscience."
- Adam Smith

"Happiness is secured through virtue; it is a good attained by man's own will."
- Thomas Aquinas

"Beauty without virtue is like a rose without scent."
- Swedish Proverb

"Virtue is harmony."
- Pythagoras

"Character is power; it makes friends, draws patronage and support and opens the way to wealth, honor and happiness."
- John Howe

## Virtue & Character

"A person's character is the sum of his or her disposition, thoughts, intentions, desires, and actions."
  - Marilyn vos Savant

"Virtue is the health of the soul."
  - Socrates

"The only true measure of success is the amount of joy we are feeling."
  - Abraham Hicks

"Virtue can only flourish among equals."
  - Mary Wollstonecraft

"Character is the basis of happiness and happiness the sanction of character."
  - George Santayana

"It is better to be hated for what you are than to be loved for what you are not."
  - André Gide

"Virtue is not the absence of vices or the avoidance of moral dangers; virtue is a vivid and separate thing, like pain or a particular smell."
  - G.K. Chesterton

"Character is like a tree and reputation like a shadow. The shadow is what we think of it; the tree is the real thing."
  - Abraham Lincoln

# Virtue & Character

"Good character is more to be praised than outstanding talent. Most talents are, to some extent, a gift. Good character, by contrast, is not given to us. We have to build it, piece by piece — by thought, choice, courage, and determination."
  - John Luther

"Every man has three characters - that which he exhibits, that which he has, and that which he thinks he has."
  - Alphonse Karr

"Character is a by-product; it is produced in the great manufacture of daily duty."
  - Woodrow Wilson

"The greatest virtues are those which are most useful to other persons."
  - Aristotle

"The greatest way to live with honor in this world is to be what we pretend to be."
  - Socrates

"Fame is a vapor, popularity an accident; riches take wings; only one thing endures, and that is character."
  - Horace Greeley

"The foundation of character is the habit of doing right in every circumstance, however trivial."
  - unknown

# Virtue & Character

"Character is like pregnancy. It cannot be hidden."
   - unknown

"The greatest accomplishment is not in never falling, but in rising again after you fall."
   - Vince Lombardi

"The most important thing in life is to decide what is most important."
   - Ken Blanchard

"The only way to truly improve your character is to be conscious of your actions and strive to do better every day."
   - unknown

"Character is the real foundation of all worthwhile success."
   - John Hays Hammond

"Virtue and genuine graces in themselves speak what no words can utter."
   - William Shakespeare

"Be more concerned with your character than your reputation, because your character is what you really are, while your reputation is merely what others think you are."
   - John Woode

"The more you practice and cultivate the virtue, the more virtuous you become, and the more you become yourself."
   - Meister Eckhart

# Virtue & Character

"Virtue is the chiefest beauty of the mind, the noblest ornament of humankind."
- Edmund Spenser

"Virtue is the only true nobility."
- Thomas Fuller

"The only true measure of a person is the quality of their character."
- Jim Rohn

"Strength of character means the ability to overcome resentment against others, to hide hurt feelings, and to forgive quickly."
- Lawrence G. Lovasik

"Virtue is the nurse of tranquility."
- Richard Cumberland

"Virtue is not a single act, but a habit of right action."
- Aristotle

# Virtue & Character

# Acknowledgments

Many thanks to Mrs. G who shared with me the value of a quote daily and inspired me to be a better version of myself.

Special thanks to my mom for always sharing quotes and her unwavering faith in the promise of a brighter tomorrow.

My sister Donna deserves an immense measure of gratitude. Her help in sorting my cascade of ideas into a coherent stream has been invaluable in this endeavor.

Also thanks to all the people imparting their wisdom in their travels into quotable gems that travel through time and land to anyone who listens. Their words, indeed, are timeless treasures for us all.

Lastly to my friends that encouraged me even during the cloudy days. Linda D., Mark J., K. Creech, S. Chesser, and Art G. - their belief and support have been the compass guiding me through these uncharted territories."

Made in the USA
Columbia, SC
13 October 2024

22a0bb14-aa31-4fa1-a0d8-3842c66578eaR01